IT SHOULDN'T HURT
TO BE A KID

Also by Patricia H. Rushford
Caring for Your Elderly Parents: The Help, Hope, and Cope Book
The Humpty Dumpty Syndrome: Putting Yourself Back
Together Again
What Kids Need Most in a Mom
Have You Hugged Your Teenager Today?
Lost in the Money Maze: Finding Your Way Through

By Jean Lush and Patricia H. Rushford
The Emotional Phases of a Woman's Life

IT SHOULDN'T HURT
TO BE A KID

PATRICIA H. RUSHFORD

SPIRE

© 1996 by Patricia H. Rushford

Published by Fleming H. Revell
a division of Baker Book House Company
P.O. Box 6287, Grand Rapids, MI 49516-6287
www.bakerbooks.com

Spire edition published 2003

Previously published in 1996 as *The Jack and Jill Syndrome: Healing for Broken Children*

Printed in the United States of America

0-8007-8705-6

Portions of chapters 7 and 8 are taken from Patricia H. Rushford, *The Humpty Dumpty Syndrome: Putting Yourself Back Together Again* (Grand Rapids: Revell, 1994).

Portions of chapters 10, 11, and 12 first appeared in Patricia H. Rushford, "Face Off," *Christian Parenting Today* (March/April 1994), 35–37.

Portions of chapter 14 on feelings and grief work first appeared in Patricia H. Rushford, "The Sad Side of Life," *Christian Parenting Today* (January/February 1992), 43; and Patricia H. Rushford, "Grief Work for Small Hearts," *Christian Parenting Today* (March/April 1992), 43.

The information and suggestions included in *The Jack and Jill Syndrome* have been extensively researched, yet this book is by no means meant to replace the expert care and advice of physicians, counselors, and therapists engaged in providing treatment to your child. Therefore, the author and publisher take no responsibility for any possible consequence of treatment or action to any child by any person reading or following the suggestions and advice offered in this book.

The characters you find in the pages of this book are real. Their names and circumstances have been altered for their protection. If you recognize yourself, it's because you are here. Everyone is here in a sense. If you don't say things like, "That sounds like me," or "It's like you've been in my house," or "This story sounds painfully familiar," I would not be doing my job as a writer.

To every child who has been broken and especially to my beloved grandchildren:

Christopher, who asked of war, "Why did it hafta happen?"

Corisa, who says, "Swinging is like a summer day."

Kyrstin, who sings, "This little light of mine, I'm gonna let it shine," and makes you believe it will shine forever.

Hannah, who said, "Guess what Nanna, I can whistle. I learned from a bird."

Jonathan, whose favorite book (at age two) was *I'll Love You Forever.*

Christian, who loves to say "no" and who, at two, is already determined to overcome adversity.

Contents

ACKNOWLEDGMENTS

For their wisdom, experience, and expertise, I'd like to thank the following critiquers, advisers, and friends:

Ron—my husband, who supported and encouraged me and who, when I was ready to break, took me on a Caribbean cruise.

Margo Power, RN—writer and mother of five.

Sandy Bjorkman—teacher, mother, and the parent of a grandchild.

Michelle Rowen, M.A.—a warm and generous counselor.

Sharon Bumala—a mom, home schooler, travel agent, and longtime political activist.

My children, David and Caryl, for bringing their children into the world and letting me share their stories.

My colleagues, who provided me with wonderful stories, case studies, and valuable insights.

The broken children I have known and loved.

Introduction

Jack and Jill went up the hill
to fetch a pail of water.
Jack fell down and broke his crown
and Jill came tumbling after.

Did you ever wonder about Jack and Jill? Oh, I know it's just a nursery rhyme, but there is a painful reality about the poem that has always bothered me. Whenever something bad happens to children, I want to know the cause. Certain questions come to mind, such as: How old were Jack and Jill? Should they have been sent to collect water? Was it an accident? Were they pushed? Were they left to fend for themselves?

As the next verse goes on to report, a nurse (possibly a nanny) did come along to wrap their heads in vinegar and brown paper— an odd cure by our standards. But it may have been the best she could offer at the time. Still, someone should have been there to protect them, to prevent the fall, or at least to carry them to safety and find out what happened at the top of the hill. And don't you think it strange that both children would meet the same fate? Perhaps an adult on the hill didn't notice them because his or her own needs were too great. Maybe someone simply wanted the children out of the way.

Like Jack and Jill, many children today fall down hills they shouldn't have to climb—hills that are far too steep and dangerous. Every day we hear about children damaged by physical abuse

11

and neglect. Sadly, even more often children are hurt on the inside, where we can't see their wounds. Yet their hearts and minds lie in shattered heaps of confusion and pain. All too often they grow up broken, reinflicting a similar kind of pain on their own children. This pervasive brokenness is a sickness, a kind of "Jack and Jill syndrome," that produces broken children generation after generation.

It Shouldn't Hurt to Be a Kid is a book about children who have been wounded by cruelties they encounter in our less-than-perfect world—cruelties such as inappropriate teasing and touching, harsh words, divorce, neglect, abandonment, and all other forms of physical, emotional, and spiritual abuse. More important, it is a book about putting lives back together again and trying to prevent future brokenness.

It's too late to help the Jack and Jill of the poem, but we can offer today's damaged children a way out of their pain. In both my personal and professional life, I have seen many people, damaged in childhood, whose pain seems to have no end. At the same time, I have seen children survive and thrive simply because someone cared enough to help.

Because of our human imperfections, we will never be perfect parents or caregivers. We can, however, teach children to cope, solve problems, and deal with the dangers. We can teach them how to survive. We can't cure all ills but we can provide good care.

Fortunately we don't have to wait until today's children are in their twenties and thirties before we work on healing their childhood wounds. We can do it now. Throughout this book we'll explore ways to turn the tide. We'll discover how to give our children the encouragement, attention, education, and love they need to become healthy, well-adjusted adults.

Part One

THE BROKEN CHILD

Children are the living messages we send
to a time we will not see.

Neil Postman

1

It Shouldn't Hurt to Be a Kid

"Oh," I gasped, clasping my hands together. "Here she comes." My daughter, Caryl, gave a final push and a little black-haired wonder slid into the doctor's waiting hands. He placed the baby on Caryl's tummy and cut the cord. The miracle of new life filled me with awe once again.

"She's adorable," I cooed as I gave the baby's mother a teary smile. Moments later the doctor placed Corisa, my first granddaughter, in my arms. She opened one eye as if to say, "Just checking," then closed it again.

My mind went back twenty some years to the day I delivered my first child. I felt an overwhelming desire to nurture and protect the little boy we named David. I wanted to keep him safe, secure, and healthy. I wanted to be the perfect parent.

As I held my granddaughter, the same thoughts flooded back, now crowded by reality. Like all parents I fell short of perfection. Although I was not an abusive parent, I made mistakes that probably left some emotional scars. I loved my children dearly and tried to keep them safe and unbroken, but I couldn't prevent their being pushed around, teased, and tormented by their peers or mishandled and misled by adults who didn't understand or didn't care. Unfortunately they had even inflicted some pain on themselves.

Like the time my children decided to hop on the back of a milk truck so they could get to school faster. It was David's idea, but Caryl chose to follow her big brother's lead. The truck started moving too fast. Caryl jumped off, scraped her knee, and hobbled back home. When I learned what had happened, I gave them a stern lecture about the dangers of hopping on milk trucks. They didn't break their crowns, but I threatened to break them if they ever pulled a stunt like that again.

They're grown now. Caryl jumped on fewer "milk trucks" and has recovered well from childhood and adolescent wounds. Sadly, David continues to suffer from wounds inflicted by himself and others. For a long time he treated his wounds with drugs and alcohol. Now he too is learning to deal with his brokenness in healthy ways.

I never meant to hurt my children, yet because of the difficulties they experienced growing up and continue to experience in adulthood, I struggled for a time with guilt and grief, knowing that I had in some way contributed to their brokenness.

"Oh, little one," I whispered softly to Corisa. "How will it be for you?" This child would go home to a loving family. She would be nurtured, adored, and cared for. But would it be enough?

Like it or not, though our family would provide a fairly safe environment, our grandchildren would probably suffer some degree of damage. I could only hope the damage wouldn't be too severe and that each child would be strong enough to overcome it.

Bad things shouldn't happen to children but they do. Every day we are reminded of the sad plight of children, not only in our country but all over the world. We've made great strides toward reform and developed stricter laws governing child safety and the rights of children. Still, millions of children end up unloved, neglected, abandoned, abused, and even murdered. Such was the case for Tavielle.

The Girl in the Window

Tavielle's mother wouldn't let her play with other children. She wasn't allowed outside. After being in kindergarten for only a month, the five-year-old girl's mother withdrew her, saying the family was moving. Neighbors later reported that they had often seen Tavielle watching them from her window.

She's gone now. According to the newspaper account, Tonia, the child's mother, had starved the child to death. She hadn't actually killed the child, Tonia explained. She'd just "let it happen." Tonia had been withholding food and water for about a month because she felt the child was "evil."[1]

It is an extreme example, I know. Yet sometimes it takes the extreme case to alert us to the dangers children in our communities face.

Ways We Fail Our Children

In our nation strict laws govern the way children are treated, but laws do little to stop the pain inflicted on children. Many children die from abuse each year—about thirteen hundred in our country. Of that number, an estimated 65 percent are under two years of age. Countless more children are damaged each year in ways we may not even know. Some sources suggest that a child is abused every forty-seven seconds in the United States.[2] Every day children suffer physical, emotional, intellectual, and spiritual abuse and neglect. Abuse occurs through abandonment, beatings, family breakup, and divorce and gradually destroys a child's self-esteem and moral character. Especially shocking is the fact that many incidents go unreported or unnoticed.

Despite the statistics, more time and money are spent in lobbying for trees, seals, and spotted owls than for children. We as a society are failing our children at nearly every level.

According to Sylvia Ann Hewlett,[3] economist and author of *When the Bough Breaks: The Cost of Neglecting Our Children,*

- Parents are spending 40 percent less time with their children than did parents twenty-five years ago.

- 42 percent of all American children between the ages of five and nine are left home alone often or at least occasionally.[4]
- More than half the children in our country have experienced the pain of losing a parent through separation or divorce.
- Fifteen million children have been abandoned by their fathers, and the rate of mothers abandoning their children has risen sharply over the last decade.
- Twelve million children in the United States lack basic health care.
- One out of five—20 percent—of our children live at or below the poverty level.
- The suicide rate among teenagers has tripled since 1970.
- About one hundred thousand children are homeless.
- An estimated one in four girls and one in ten boys are sexually abused by the time they reach eighteen.

As Hillary Clinton says in her book *It Takes a Village,*

... everywhere we look, children are under assault: from violence and neglect, from the breakup of families, from the temptations of alcohol, tobacco, sex, and drug abuse, from greed, materialism, and spiritual emptiness. These problems are not new, but in our time they have skyrocketed. Against this bleak backdrop, the struggle to raise strong children and to support families, emotionally as well as practically, has become more fierce.[5]

Like Jack and Jill, far too many children fall, often breaking more than their crowns. If they survive their ordeals, they may lose the ability to trust and to think for themselves. Many live in fear. Some become enraged. Most are crippled physically, emotionally, or spiritually.

One woman, who had been broken as a child, wisely said:

It shouldn't hurt to be a kid. We must listen to children, protect them and nurture them. I sometimes wonder how different my life would have been if there had been someone in my childhood who was able to hear me, be with me, protect me. Someone who could have asked, "Honey, has someone hurt you?"[6]

Each one of us is called to be that someone to the Jacks and Jills of this world.

For Those Who Care

If you're reading this book, chances are you are struggling to care for or assist in the care of a child who has been broken in some way. You may have caused the damage, or it may have been caused by a family member, relative, friend, teacher, babysitter, or stranger. You may know exactly what happened and understand why the child is acting out and is difficult to manage.

Angie, for example, cares for her son, who was neglected by his biological father and suffered emotional and physical abuse at the hands of Angie's second husband. Angie struggles daily under a load of guilt because she didn't stop the abuse sooner.

Jennifer also cares for a damaged child. Her daughter, Tammy, seemed well-adjusted and happy during her early childhood. Then at age ten, Tammy changed. "She ignores the rules, gets poor grades, is mouthy and rebellious, and has run away three times." Now, at twelve, she has a boyfriend and is sexually active. Jennifer says, "I've tried everything to turn her around. I don't know what happened. All I know is I have to find a way to stop this madness."

Abused by the System

Sometimes we are left to care for children damaged by the very system designed to protect them. One story that comes to mind is that of Denise, a single mother, and her daughter. The child was reportedly removed from her mother's care by Children Services because Denise had chosen to continue breastfeeding, even though the child was two years old. Denise, having been wrongly accused of abuse, fought to get her daughter back and a year later won her case. But her healthy and happy baby had been broken.

The once outgoing and talkative toddler returned a "... clingy little girl who fears strangers, cries out in her sleep, and wants to be cuddled constantly."

"Mommy," the child cries, "my heart has been so empty of you because you weren't there. Please hold me. Fill my heart back up."[7]

Grandparents Who Parent

Perhaps you are one of the estimated four million grandparents parenting grandchildren.[8] After rearing three children, Marion and Harry thought they would settle into a quiet and comfortable midlife. It never happened. Their youngest daughter, Becky, started drinking and using drugs in her early teens. She married but her marriage ended in divorce, and Becky returned to her parents' home to have her first baby. Miraculously, Todd was born healthy.

Shortly after giving birth to Todd, Becky married a second time and became pregnant again. This time she used cocaine during her pregnancy and her second baby was born drug-affected. During this time, Todd suffered numerous questionable injuries. Marion and Harry suspected abuse and reported their suspicions to authorities. Following a complicated legal battle, the courts granted them custody of the children. Now they are trying to adjust to the changes in their lifestyle as they try to pick up the pieces of their grandchildren's fractured lives.

We Can Make a Difference

Caring for broken children is, at times, a monumental task, yet, with compassion, love, and hope we can make a difference in these children's lives.

Mental health centers and children services departments are crowded with children of all ages who act out their anger, fears, insecurities, and pain by hurting themselves or others. While counseling can help both parents and children, it is those within the family and community who are with the children most often—

parents, grandparents, guardians, teachers, and caregivers—who can make the greatest difference.

As a book written for those who care about children, *It Shouldn't Hurt to Be a Kid* takes an honest and realistic look at children and the dangers inherent in being a child. We'll examine such questions as:

- How and by whom are children broken?
- How can we be the parents and caregivers that children need?
- How do we cope with a "difficult" child?
- What happens when love isn't enough?
- How can we teach children to help themselves?
- What can we do to keep children safe?
- How can we help damaged children find hope and healing?
- How can we create a supportive community, giving children and the adults who care for them a brighter future?

We are not always aware of the pain we inflict on children. This may be due in part to our adult views and values—our hurts, prejudices, and insecurities. We may not understand the world from a child's perspective because we've lost our own childlike qualities along the way. We've forgotten how it feels to be a child. When children are deeply or repeatedly hurt, the joys of childhood fade into the pain of feeling devalued and unloved. Children in pain often become enraged adolescents and adults who turn against themselves and society.

Ultimately our goal will be to help children feel valued. M. Scott Peck, in his book *The Road Less Traveled*, says, "When children know that they are valued, when they truly feel valued in the deepest parts of themselves, then they feel valuable. This knowledge is worth more than any gold."[9]

How do we value children? How do we put broken children back together again? The first step is to understand how we devalue or wound them. This is covered in the next two chapters. As you read about how children become broken, you may feel uncomfortable at times. The stories and illustrations may be painfully similar to your child's experiences or to your own. Perhaps you will feel grief or guilt as you realize you have had a hand in hurting a child. You may also feel angry or defensive as you discover ways in which adults knowingly, and sometimes unknowingly, wound children.

I want to assure you that this is not another parent-bashing book. Since I am a less-than-perfect parent myself, I don't intend to accuse or criticize. My aim is to bring relief and forgiveness—to offer hope and healing to broken children of every age.

2

CHILDREN AND THE PEOPLE
WHO BREAK THEM

If I asked you to draw a picture of a child breaker, what would he or she look like? Would you draw a picture of the boy next door or the new mother down the street? Would he or she look like a mother, father, grandparent, teacher, doctor, pastor or priest, police officer, social worker, Uncle John, or Aunt Jane? Probably not, unless, of course, you or your child experienced abuse at the hands of one of these people. Often we imagine a child abuser to be a person who has lost his or her mind to drugs or alcohol. When I picture someone who breaks children, I immediately think of Wesley Allen Dodd, a child molester.

Dodd stood in the courtroom with his hands cuffed behind his back. The words uttered by the newscasters—"child molester, pedophile, murderer"—didn't seem to fit the picture of the shy, average-looking, young man standing there. Authorities had charged him with the sexual assault and murder of three little boys in the Portland/Vancouver area.

Another example of people who break children is the father in the following story.

23

"Father Kills Tot in Custody War," the headlines screamed. Anger and grief swept through me as I read the horrifying story of a thirty-six-year-old man who had killed his daughter and then doused himself with gasoline and set himself on fire. In the ambulance, in a matter-of-fact way, he reported to police that he had killed his daughter because he didn't want his wife to get custody of her.

According to the police officer, the child's father had "smothered her and . . . knew she was dead because he took her pulse about fifteen minutes before he set himself on fire." The father died nine hours later.

The newspaper photo showed a tiny body lying on the ground while a police officer on the scene worked to revive her. Apparently the rampage had begun the day before, after a meeting with the wife's divorce attorney. That night he threatened his wife with a knife and bound her with duct tape. He forced her to write a will saying she would give up custody of her children. She escaped and raced to a neighbor for help. After the tragedy, the couple's four-year-old son told police, "Daddy put my sister in the garbage."

Most of us can look at these cases and say, yes, these are the kind of people who break children. I used to think of people who break children as animals—subhuman, evil beings, monsters who prey on the innocent. If I didn't look too closely, I could separate them from the rest of the human race. Yet, as I have looked at their faces and listened to their stories, I have realized that they are not really all that different from you and me.

While we may find a villainous-looking character playing the part in a movie, in real life people who break children look all too familiar. If you had met Wesley Allen Dodd on the street, you probably would not have recognized him as an abuser. He was tried, convicted, and hanged for his heinous crimes. At the hanging some people cheered. I watched it on television and cried. I had seen his face and heard his story.

Wesley Allen Dodd was more than a villain who broke children. He was a tormented man who had been abused as a child. He hated what he'd become and begged society to kill him.

People who break children are not only criminals; they are often our friends, relatives, neighbors, and sometimes ourselves. Child breakers have a human face and that face could be the one looking back at us from our own mirrors.

Children Reflect Their World

I first noticed our son's brokenness when he was in the fourth grade. He came home with the packet of photos a photographer had taken at school. I suppose I must have known that something was wrong before that, but somehow it didn't register until then. In the photos of past years he always had an impish grin. His eyes shone with the joy of just being a kid.

But these photos were different. The smile had been replaced with a look of what? anger? cynicism? It was hard to pinpoint. But in my mother's heart, I knew something had gone wrong. I tried to counter it with all the good parenting tricks I knew.

When he hit his teens, his condition worsened. He ran away, was arrested, started drinking. Like any parent, I wondered why. What happened to my child? Who did this to him? Was it me? My husband? Had we disciplined too harshly—not enough? Was it the school? his peers? society as a whole?

Who had broken my child? At first I tried to place the blame on others, then on myself. I even blamed God a time or two before realizing how futile the blame game can be.

As it turns out, there is really no individual or group to blame. He made wrong choices, my husband and I made mistakes, but much of the difficulty turned out to be biological in nature. We recently learned that my son has a bi-polar disorder or what is more commonly known as manic-depression. Today he is on medications that help him control his symptoms. My son was broken primarily by a condition that causes a chemical imbalance in the brain.

While genetics can sometimes play a part in how a child turns out, so too does the environment in which he grows up. We all— individually and as a community—play a part in how kids turn out. Children, like art, are a reflection of life.

The Imitators

Children learn certain behaviors by imitating the people around them. Just the other day I was playing—one of my favorite pastimes—with an infant. I smiled; he smiled. I formed an O with my mouth and opened my eyes wide. He did the same.

Years ago I discovered a well-known poem that brings home the principle of imitation.

> *A Child Lives What He Learns*
> If a child lives with criticism,
> He learns to condemn.
> If a child lives with hostility,
> He learns to fight.
> If a child lives with shame,
> He learns to feel guilty.
> If a child lives with tolerance,
> He learns to be patient.
> If a child lives with encouragement,
> He learns confidence.
> If a child lives with praise,
> He learns to appreciate.
> If a child lives with fairness,
> He learns justice.
> If a child lives with security,
> He learns to have faith.
> If a child lives with approval,
> He learns to like himself.
> If a child lives with acceptance and friendship,
> He learns to find love in the world.
>
> Dorothy Law Nolte

Children learn from and imitate not only positive traits and actions, but also the negative, inappropriate, immoral, and dangerous things they see people do. In a movie several boys stretched out on the centerline of a busy road, as a test of either their manhood or their stupidity—I forget which. The boys in the movie survived. Unfortunately, the movie stunt was repeated in real life. One young man was killed and another seriously injured.

Violent Imaginings

One of my greatest concerns these days is the way children are reflecting the violence and hostility so prevalent in the world. There has always been violence, but sadly, with the production of certain video games, television shows, movies, and books, violence has become big business.

The majority of our children, of course, are not violent and will grow up to be responsible human beings who do not pose a threat to themselves or others. But as William J. Bennett says in the article "What to Do about the Children," "The condition of too many of our children is not good." According to Bennett,

- From 1960 to 1991 the rate of homicide deaths among children under the age of nineteen more than quadrupled. Among black teenagers, homicide is now by far the leading cause of death.
- Since 1965 the juvenile arrest rate for violent crimes has tripled, and the fastest growing segment of the criminal population is made up of children.
- Since 1960 the rate at which teenagers take their own lives has more than tripled.[1]

Just as toxic waste spoils our environment, unharnessed violence ravages the hearts and souls of our young by destroying their value for human life and polluting their minds.

In her article "Children's Violent Imaginings Reflect Unhealthy Society," writer Donna Britt shared her concerns and those of teachers she had interviewed about the violent thoughts and stories of grade school children. It used to be that children expressed their "anger, fears, and insecurity in phrases like, 'I'm going to punch him in the stomach.'"[2]

Today the stories are macabre—even those of children who come from nonviolent backgrounds. Today's heroes and villains pull out eyes, chop off arms, and decapitate their victims. They use guns and knives and other lethal weapons. Through cable television and videos the horrifying world of such movies as *Terminator II* and *Silence of the Lambs* is available to young children.

Many children play video games where characters are tortured, maimed, and killed, with blood spurting out of severed body parts. As Britt indicates, the world has always had its share of scary stories, but "there has never been a time when children who were not living in a war zone navigated their way through as much murder and mayhem. Violent media images aren't real. But the stories [written by children today] suggest that for many kids, the culture itself feels like a battlefield."[3]

Images remain in our minds for a long time. Whatever we hear or experience enters our brains and takes up residence. Have you ever had a thought, word, or song that wouldn't go away? It is especially annoying and perhaps even harmful if the image that won't go away is obscene or vulgar. Brian Horvath, a teacher, said, "If you eat bad food, you become unhealthy. If you experience a bad psychological environment, the outcome is negative. And there's so much negativity from all avenues that it's hard for a third grader to maintain his naivete—or just his view that the world is a positive place."[4]

We as a society damage children by exposing them to megadoses of violence. A *USA Today* article tells us that "almost half of young adults witnessed an act of violence last year, and nearly a fourth were crime victims."[5] But we don't need statistics. All we have to do is turn on the news.

Violence breeds violence. Aggression breeds aggression. Childhood innocence and delight in life are being distorted by images children see in movies, on television, and in video games—even in their own homes. If we continually expose children to this kind of violence, we too are guilty of child abuse.

We Are All Guilty

Children live what they learn. Sad, but so very true. Most of us don't set out to hurt children. Yet nearly every child has suffered some damage and nearly every adult has mistreated a child.

Perhaps you can recall times when you were deeply hurt as a child. And as an adult, you can probably remember damaging a child—times when you may have reacted too harshly, punished too severely, said words that cut too deeply, or not taken a child's perceptions or feelings seriously. I certainly can.

When we treat our children in any way that does not conform to God's will or standards, we are, on some level, abusive. Hurting children, in any way, is outside God's plan for humanity. Abuse, in any form and against anyone, is a sin against that individual. It is an act that truly damages self and others, and as such it is an offense against God and the human conscience.[6]

God's plan for us is holiness and wholeness. We were created to relate perfectly to God, ourselves, and one another. Any word or action that falls short of that perfection carries with it a potential for brokenness.

As Dr. Brian W. Grant, author of *From Sin to Wholeness*, says, we hurt others when "whatever we do or are . . . destroys, for ourselves or another, the reality or possibility of life lived in communion with God, whether we acknowledge that fact or not. We can substitute many words for 'destroys'—including 'delays', 'diminishes', 'obstructs', or 'dilutes'. All identify acts that interfere with an individual's state of peace with one's neighbor and oneself, the natural world and our Creator."[7]

Grant goes on to say that he believes "a person is happiest when that peace is achieved" and that "any sin against God also produces dislocation and unhappiness in the human realm for at least the sinner, and often for many others as well."[8]

How do we know when a child has been broken? *A child is broken when someone in authority uses his or her power to cause pain or to somehow diminish or devalue that child.* In using this definition we must come to terms with the fact that we are all, to some degree, people who break children.

At this point, some of you may be saying, "Wait a minute. Something is wrong here. I may have made some mistakes, but I certainly don't go around abusing children."

Certainly there is a big difference between blatant abuse and human error, and I don't want to minimize the problem of child abuse. Unfortunately our children can't always discern that difference. We'll talk more about that later.

First, though, you may want to reflect on any damage you may have caused a child in your care. Whenever we injure someone, we need to deal with the guilt, confess whatever wrong we've committed, ask God for forgiveness, and make amends when we can.

Dealing with Guilt

As you read this book, you may from time to time feel guilty for things you've done or neglected to do in the past. In this sense, guilt is not a bad thing because it brings us to the place where we recognize our sins and shortcomings. We can then call on God to forgive us. Just as we have all sinned and fallen short of God's glory—of perfection, we have all made mistakes in dealing with children.

If you feel you have wronged a child along the way, stop, confess any wrongdoing to God, and, if it's appropriate, to the child. Then put the problem behind you and move on. It may help to write down your offenses as they come to you; then pray over each one, crossing it out as you thank God for his mercy and grace. Trust that God has forgiven you and forgive yourself.

Guilt can defeat you if you dwell on it. It can erode your confidence and lessen your ability to provide good care. Don't allow yourself to become so guilt-ridden that it keeps you from effectively caring for and nurturing your children. Instead, hold firm to this Bible verse: "If we confess our sins, [God] is faithful and just to forgive us our sins, and to cleanse us from all unrighteousness" (1 John 1:9 KJV).

Now, with our sins forgiven, let's move into the next chapter and take a look at brokenness from a child's perspective.

3

SEE ALL THE BROKEN CHILDREN

Do you hear the children weeping
Oh my brothers?

Elizabeth Barrett Browning
The Cry of the Children

I met eight-year-old Joshua while interning for my master's degree in counseling. His father had routinely beaten him and his mother. Night after night he lay in his bed trying not to feel the pain in his own body, trying not to listen to the noises coming from his parents' room—the loud bangs, the sickening thuds, his mother's cries and muted screams. The thin wall dulled the noise some, but the horror of his father's brutality pierced his heart with bull's-eye accuracy. His mother finally gained the courage to leave her abusive husband, but Joshua lives in terror that Dad will find and kill them.

"Dads are supposed to love their kids," he says in a melancholy voice. A few minutes later he tears around the room with his toy assault rifle. "He'd better not come around here. I'm going to blow his head off." He pulls the trigger and waves the gun back and forth. The gun rat-ta-tats. I close my eyes and pray that my little client won't someday get a real gun, with real bullets.

Two-year-old Cassie's mother strapped Cassie into the high chair, determined to teach her how to eat without making a mess. Adelle didn't understand that it's normal for children to make messes. She hit Cassie for spilling food, for wetting the bed, for leaving her toys on the floor. She didn't want a child who gave her any trouble. In truth Adelle didn't want a child at all. Oh, she hadn't felt that way at first. Adelle had wanted to get pregnant. She had the notion a baby would be a sweet, lovable doll who would love her and fill the aching void inside. Of course that didn't happen.

Fortunately an uncle intervened, took Cassie home, and called Children Services to report the abuse. CSD placed Cassie with foster parents who later adopted her. Adelle seemed relieved as she signed papers giving up Cassie. I was relieved as well. Perhaps now Cassie would have a chance.

Amy's biological father left home when she was five. When she turned ten, her mother married again. Amy's stepfather sexually assaulted her and her older sister. They told Aunt Lucy. The stepfather was tried, sentenced, and paroled. Amy's mother abandoned her children to live with this sex offender.

"I can handle the sexual abuse," Amy said. "I know he can't touch me anymore, but . . ." Tears filled her doe-brown eyes. "What really hurts is that my mother chose him over me."

Peter's mom and dad do drugs. When they go out to party, they lock seven-year-old Peter in the closet and leave his eighteen-month-old sister alone in her crib. They don't think Peter is old enough to take care of his sister. He leans his head on his arms and rests against his knees, determined not to cry. He used to beat against the door, hoping it would open so he could go and comfort his little sister. Now he just sits in silent rage and closes his ears to her screams. Someday they'll be sorry.

Joshua, Cassie, Amy, and Peter are all victims of child abuse and neglect. But let's look for a moment at another kind of abuse—the kind we don't always see. To those outside the home and perhaps even to their parents, these children may act like they're doing fine. Every day, however, the painful hammer of criticism shatters their self-esteem.

"What's the matter with you, Michael?" Mom scolded. "Can't you do anything right?" She was on him again, this time for the way he'd cleaned his room. "Why can't you learn to pick up your things?" she asked as she remade the bed he'd worked so hard on. "You're seven years old, for heaven's sake. Stop acting like such a baby. It's about time you start acting your age."

Yesterday Mom was upset about the letter from school. Michael hadn't been doing so well in reading and math lately. He tried, but sometimes it was just too hard to think. Day before that, he'd struck out at T-ball practice. Dad had yelled at him for that.

Michael sat on his bed and rubbed his head. "Guess I must really be bad," he murmured aloud. "Bet my folks wish they had somebody else as their kid and not me. Bet if I ran away from home, they wouldn't even miss me." Michael didn't want to run away. He liked his house and his dog. He even liked his mom and dad—most of the time. Maybe he would just have to try harder to be good, he decided, so they could like him more.

We don't know what will happen to these children as they grow up and become adults. Will they heal? While they may patch up their broken lives and make the best of things, will they ever be healthy and whole? Chances are, unless they get the kind of help they need, they will be broken, needy adults.

I spoke with Maggie, who, as a child, was devastated by her parents' divorce. "I'm still affected by the divorce and by my mother's attitude toward me. Funny thing is Mom hasn't a clue. She's always seen herself as a model mother. It wouldn't have done any good to tell her otherwise."

The Reaction of Children

In broken children, we not only find various forms of abuse—physical, sexual, emotional, intellectual, and spiritual—but we also find varying ways in which children react to the wrongs done to them. To learn how and why children break, we'll want to look at each child's:

- *perception* or how he or she sees the situation
- *personality* or temperament
- *vulnerability*
- *resilience* and the ability to cope

Perception

Adults may believe they are acting in the best interests of a child. Their actions, however, may permanently traumatize the child. Let me give you an example. I recall an incident that hurt me deeply when I was about two, maybe three. My mother had put me to bed and forgotten to give me a good-night kiss.

I cried for her to come back. She did, but not to kiss me. Instead, she angrily insisted I go to sleep. I don't remember if Mom spanked me but I do remember that I curled up in the dark and cried myself to sleep.

My mother doesn't recall the incident. Perhaps she'd kissed me earlier in the evening and I'd forgotten. I may have gone through the whole bedtime routine—needing water, going potty, and running out of excuses. I don't know. She may have done nothing wrong. In fact she was probably following good parenting rules by being consistent, firm, and diligent in not giving in to my demands.

Yet as a child, I was heartbroken and at times the memory still haunts me. My mother did not purposely abuse me, but for that space in time I felt lonely, rejected, and unloved. This was my perception. The child in me had been wounded.

I'm sure you can think of situations or events in your childhood that hurt you as well.

John has low self-esteem. He feels worthless and as a result has difficulty keeping a job. He's been married and divorced four times and has spent years dropping in and out of counseling programs.

"The problem," John insists, "stems from my father. He was always belittling and criticizing me. He'd say things like, 'That was good, but you can do better.' I think I'm still trying to impress him."

At one point he confronted his dad. "My father just looked at me with his mouth open. He didn't know what I was talking about. He said he loved me and was only trying to make a man out of me. In fact the way he said it made me feel like any misunderstanding was my fault."

John, at least the little boy in John, doesn't feel loved. He feels betrayed and useless.

In another case, Sandra said, "I've always had trouble with my weight. When I was younger, my father called me names like 'Hippo-hips,' 'Rhino-rump,' or 'bucket-of-lard.'" Sandra told me of a time her father stopped the car and said, "Well, looks like you'll have to get out." When she asked why, he pointed to a road sign that said, LOAD LIMIT 10 TONS. "The car weighs five tons, and with you in here, we're over the limit."

"I cried, but Mom and Dad just laughed and told me I shouldn't be so sensitive. It was just a joke." The child in Sandra still feels the pain of being the brunt of those cruel and senseless "jokes." Sandra went on to say, "Some of us suffer for years before we hit the point where we can say, 'I was abused as a child but now I must stop mistreating myself. I need to make choices that will help me overcome my problems, not add to them.'"

Kevin suffered a traumatic childhood. His parents both drank and eventually his father left. At age eleven Kevin was working at a part-time job after school and often taking care of his little sister. "It was tough, but that's life," he now says. "There's no point crying over it. My folks were pretty good to me when they were sober. It would have been nice to have had a normal family, but, hey, I handled it."

The perceptions of children, though they may not always be an accurate interpretation of events, are, nonetheless, very real.

35

Personality

Another variable to consider is the personality or temperament of the child. Personality greatly influences our responses to the way people treat us and it influences the way we treat ourselves.

Sharon has two children, Robert and Amanda. At seven, Robert is into everything. Even when he knows he'll get a spanking, he sometimes deliberately disobeys. Once he brought his collection of snakes into the house and let them loose in his sister's room. He then went to his room to put on extra pairs of shorts and jeans to pad his bottom. Returning to the scene of the crime, he confessed and announced he was ready for his punishment. Later, he rubbed his sore bottom, thinking, with a sly grin on his face, that seeing the look on his sister's and mother's faces when they encountered the snakes was definitely worth the pain of a spanking.

Four-year-old Amanda, on the other hand, has had only one spanking yet is terrified of being hit. A scolding is enough to send her into depression for days. She is extremely sensitive and easily hurt. We don't know how Amanda will perceive her childhood, but let's hope she's able to weather the storms ahead by developing resilience. And let's hope Robert quits terrorizing her.

Vulnerability

The degree to which a child suffers may depend on how vulnerable he or she is at any given time. For example, Shelly's vulnerability level is very high. Her parents are going through a divorce. Grief, self-blame, and stress make her more susceptible to being hurt by things that ordinarily wouldn't phase her. Her mother's annoyance at her for not picking up her clothes may make her feel unloved. A broken promise by her father may lead to her feeling unimportant and unwanted.

Resilience

Closely related to personality are resilience and the ability to cope. Some individuals have a built-in ability to "roll with the punches" so to speak. They manage to adapt to their circumstances and seem to recover from trauma with few residual effects.

Andy, for example, received frequent beatings from his mother. She would leave him alone for hours in the evening—sometimes all night while she went out with boyfriends and partied. After a neighbor found the boy alone (Andy was then four), she called Children Services and reported the incident.

Authorities placed Andy in a foster home with a loving couple who later adopted him. At first, Andy was frightened and would cringe every time anyone approached him. After a couple of months, Andy relaxed and soon became a bubbly, outgoing child. Today, at fifteen, Andy continues to be warm, outgoing, and friendly and is able to cope with difficult situations.

Not all children have this kind of resilience. Some are easily wounded and defeated, unable to bounce back. We'll be talking more in a later chapter about the resiliency factor and how to help children develop it.

What Does It Take?

What does it take to break a child? Or, perhaps more appropriately, what does it take for a child to feel broken? I've known people who survived terrible physical, sexual, and emotional abuse and neglect as children, who have grown into productive, well-adjusted adults. I have also known those who fell apart after one negative experience.

It can happen. I remember feeling self-confident as a child. Yet in my teens I struggled with low self-esteem. Why? It wasn't anything my parents did or said. It was an eighth-grade teacher. I went to school the first day after Christmas vacation wearing a beautiful new red sweater. To complete my new look, I'd used matching red lipstick.

My teacher told me I looked ridiculous. At least that's what I heard. I can't remember her exact words. She probably never meant to hurt my feelings. She may have only wanted to help me preserve my youth, perhaps feeling that bright red lipstick was not appropriate for someone my age. But she did hurt me. To this day, when I wear lipstick, it is generally a light color. When I try a darker shade, I look at myself in the mirror, and that eighth-grade girl in me hears the critical voice say, "You look ridiculous." Then I wipe it off.

It didn't devastate me or ruin my life. Today I realize self-esteem goes much deeper than the color of my lips. Yet, on occasion, it still manages to adversely affect the way I see myself.

Some of these examples may seem like minor infractions in the whole scheme of things. Yet to the child, a harsh word can have as painful an effect as a bullet taken during a raid by enemy soldiers. In fact the impact is often greater, for a bullet might be a random thing, whereas words are deliberately aimed shots of betrayal by those who claim to love you.

Each child is unique. Each comes to us with a different set of perceptions, temperament, and personality. Each has differing degrees of vulnerability and resiliency and different ways in which he or she learns to cope with life. As we care for children, we'll want to be aware of these differences and be flexible and understanding in the way we handle each child.

You may want to take a few moments and write down your impressions of each child in your care. Note their differences, the way in which they respond to you and others, as well as how they handle difficult circumstances and problems.

To help you do this I recommend the book *Different Children Different Needs: The Art of Adjustable Parenting* by Charles F. Boyd and David Boehi. The authors include a personality assessment system to help you determine how each child is motivated and they tell you how to tailor your parenting style to meet each child's needs.

Speaking of parenting styles, in part 2, "Being the Parent Your Child Needs," we'll discover what it takes to be a good parent, learn to think more objectively, assess our parenting skills, determine our children's needs, and learn how to relate to children in healthier, more loving ways.

Being the parent or caregiver your child needs entails careful consideration of who you are and how you react to your kids. You may want to ask yourself:

- Am I responding to my children in healthy ways?
- Am I letting my needs overshadow the needs of my children?
- Am I hurting my children?

In the next chapter we'll be looking at specific parenting pitfalls and discover how some adult problems can adversely affect children.

Part Two

BEING THE PARENT YOUR CHILD NEEDS

The most important part of our happiness comes not from what we have but from how we live with those we love.

Source unknown

4

PARENTING PITFALLS

"I wasn't a very good parent," my friend Betty admitted. "When I was a child, I suffered a lot of emotional abuse. Oh, it wasn't anything you could see, and now I realize my parents didn't know any better. It's taken me forty years to come to the point where I feel validated as a person."

"What do you think caused you to feel that way?" I asked.

Betty shrugged. "I can't even think of any specific things they said. I only know I never felt like I was good enough for them." She paused for a moment and added, "Dad had an anger problem, and I remember Mom would always be really careful not to set him off. If he did explode, Mom would get mad at one of us kids. It was always something we did wrong. But you know what probably hurt even worse was that they never ever told me I was okay. They never praised me or gave me compliments—*that* might have made me conceited."

"Earlier you said you didn't feel you were a good parent. How did being emotionally damaged as a child affect your parenting?"

"I imitated my folks—I even married an abusive husband. I shudder to think how hurtful I was to my kids. I swore I'd do things differently but I ended up abusing them in a lot of the same ways. I don't care what anyone says, if you don't respect yourself—if you don't love and value yourself—you're not going to respect, love, and value your kids."

Through counseling, a support group, and a deepening relationship with God, Betty has learned how to take care of herself and in the process is better able to care for others. Her children are grown, but as Betty has admitted to them her mistakes and asked their forgiveness, she and her children have become close. She's getting a second chance in a way by being a doting grandmother to her five grandchildren. Together she and her family are recognizing their mistakes and breaking the abuse cycle.

Danger Zones

Did you ever want to run away from home? Do you ever feel like you're ready to explode? Have you ever blown up at your children? Have you abused your kids? Are you afraid you might? As we've seen, broken parents don't always treat their kids or themselves in appropriate ways. Even healthy parents can find themselves in situations where they are in danger of losing control.

In this chapter we're going to look at certain circumstances or danger zones that can lead to child abuse. The idea here is not to make excuses for inappropriate acts, but to be aware of certain pitfalls. Then if you find you have a problem, acknowledge it and work toward resolution.

A Physical Problem

Linda cuddled her newborn to her breast. Tender warmth wrapped its soothing blanket around her. She was a mother. For nine months she'd waited for this moment. "Karen Elizabeth," she whispered as she lightly touched the tiny face and traced her daughter's delicate features with her forefinger. "You are the most beautiful baby in the world."

One week later, Linda walked the floor with Karen. Her wonderful baby had been crying with colic for three hours. Suddenly something snapped inside. Her grip on the infant tightened. She slapped Karen's bottom. "Just shut up!" she screamed and hit her again. Karen cried harder.

Terrified by the anger exploding inside her, Linda put Karen in the bassinet. "I'm sorry, baby," she gasped. "I didn't mean to hurt you. But I can't . . ."

Karen wailed even louder. Linda pressed a hand to the baby's mouth. "Please," she hissed through her tightly set jaw, "stop crying before I . . ."

Linda shrank from the murderous thoughts racing through her mind. She clenched her fists and ran into the bathroom and locked the door. There she gripped the counter and stared at the tear-stained image in the mirror. *What is wrong with you?* The condemning voice roared in her head. *What kind of mother are you?* Linda drew in a ragged breath and ran a hand through her disheveled hair. Never in her life had she experienced such feelings of rage. And toward a baby! In that terrible moment as she stood beside Karen's bed, Linda had envisioned herself pressing harder and harder until she'd silenced the child forever.

Linda turned away from the image. She'd always seen herself as an attractive woman, slender, with dark hair and sky blue eyes. She'd pictured herself as a loving wife and doting mother. Yet a moment ago she had looked into the eyes of a mad woman, a woman who had nearly killed her baby, a woman who had slapped a newborn.

Frightened by the experience, Linda sought help. Her doctor diagnosed postpartum depression.[1] He placed her on medication and suggested she get someone to help her care for the baby for a while. Within a few weeks, Linda's depression had passed and she was able to give her baby the kind of care she needed. Sometimes a medical problem can affect the way we think about and react to our children. If you suspect that may be a problem for you, call your doctor and see a counselor.

Social Isolation

Kristen, a young mother of four, rarely left home. She and her husband decided she should be a stay-at-home mom and take care of the children. She had few friends and a limited social life. She rarely took time away from the children. Isolation sent Kristen into a deep depression. She often felt out of control, angry, and resentful, and her children suffered as a result.

Some parents place themselves and their children at risk by deliberately isolating themselves from community and family members. Perhaps I should offer a word of explanation here. When I say social isolation, I'm not talking about parents who home school or about keeping children out of compromising social situations. I'm referring to people who close themselves away from practically all contact with the outside world. This often happens in abusive homes. The husband may be beating his wife and children. To keep the family secret intact, he insists on their right to privacy and tries to keep others out of his home and away from his family.

Avoid the dangers social isolation can bring by being an active member of the community. Open your doors regularly to family, friends, and neighbors.

Inadequate Parenting Skills

Sometimes children are broken simply because parents don't know any better. While I worked as a pediatric nurse, I encountered several children with injuries caused by parents who didn't realize that lifting a child by the arm could dislocate the shoulder. Other parents have left babies on dressing tables only for a moment and had them roll off. One mother left her two year old in the bathtub alone for a minute to answer the phone—the baby drowned. Many children die in accidents that could have been prevented if their parents had only known the dangers.

Caring for children is a difficult job, yet parents are expected to simply step into the role as though they'd been thoroughly trained. Most have not. Many parents, even though they may be highly intelligent and well-educated, are inadequately equipped to rear children. They desperately need support from other adults—in the family, church, or community.

The problem of inadequate parenting skills can be easily remedied. Most communities offer parenting classes, and the library is full of books and magazines on the subject. In fact, you're reading one of them now.

Lack of Support

Do your children ever get to be more than you can handle? Could you use a break? Is there someone you can call when your kids are getting to you and you need to get away?

We all need someone we can call when we're reaching a breaking point—or when we want advice. We need to be able to express our fears and concerns freely to someone who understands and who can model healthy relational and parenting skills.

To learn more about support systems for parents, see chapter 16.

Marital Problems

Andre stretched out on his son's bed to read a bedtime story. His four year old, Nathan, snuggled closer and rested his head against Dad's broad chest. On the surface everything looks fine—a nurturing dad spending time with his son.

Nathan loved the story, and afterward they said prayers, then Andre tucked Nathan in and gave him a good-night kiss. As Andre closed the door, his son called out, "Daddy, will we ever get to see Mommy again?"

Andre tightened his grip on the door handle. It had been six months since his daring escape. It wasn't a path he would have chosen, but what else could he do? His wife hadn't wanted to share custody of Nathan. The only way Andre could see his son was to snatch him and run. "I don't know, son," Andre finally answered. "Mommy doesn't want us anymore." Then stepping back into the room, he cradled the boy in his arms. "So I guess it's just you and me."

"Did I be too bad, Daddy?" Nathan asked.

"No," Andre said quickly. "I told you before, Nathan, it wasn't your fault. It's no one's fault."

Nathan doesn't understand. He is confused and worried. He only knows he must have done something terribly wrong if Mommy doesn't love him anymore.

Nathan's pain won't show up as bruises, at least not where you can see them. He's caught in the middle of a custody battle. In these battles children are often bartered like furniture. The stakes are high and nobody wins.

Those who suffer most in marital problems are the children. They may suffer physical abuse by parents who take out their anger and frustration on them. Usually, however, the most damaging effects of divorce are emotional.

As writer David Neff says in his article "The Painless-divorce Myth," many children damaged by divorce go into adulthood unable to form lasting bonds, still dragging along emotional baggage such as fear, sadness, anger, guilt, and grief.[2] "Even when children experience an immediate sense of relief because parental squabbles have been cut off," says Neff, "the sense of abandonment can be crippling."[3]

I don't mean to condemn or criticize those parents who are experiencing marital problems or divorce. I know some parents who are doing an excellent job of caring for their children through the trauma. Despite the care that the adults take, however, the child will probably suffer, and the adults should get counseling to help the family deal with the trauma.

Substance Abuse

Children whose parents use drugs and/or alcohol are considered to be at a high risk for abuse. Damage to children can occur in several ways. Mothers who take drugs or drink alcoholic beverages during pregnancy are passing the damaging substances on to their babies. These drugs can and often do produce drug-affected children. Babies may be born addicted to drugs or be incapacitated by fetal alcohol syndrome or other major physical, mental, and behavioral problems.

Alcohol and drug use have long been linked to domestic violence. Substance abuse is a factor in approximately 40 percent of all child abuse cases. The use of these substances can impair judgment and the ability to reason and think clearly. According to

Lorette Kowel, of the Massachusetts Society for the Prevention of Cruelty to Children, "Crack can turn a loving mother into a monster in ten minutes."[4]

In 1986, 262,000 children throughout the United States were in substitute (or foster) care, while today there are about half a million. Most child welfare experts attribute this astounding increase to drug abuse by parents.[5]

Don't subject your children to the kind of trauma substance abuse produces. If you are one of the many parents who struggle with drug and/or alcohol addiction, get help today.

Unrealistic Expectations

Christie is a successful lawyer. She has high standards and wants what's best for her family. She expects her children to be orderly and obedient and will not tolerate what she considers bad behavior. Unfortunately much of that behavior is simply being a child.

Unrealistic expectations can often be seen in individuals who want more from their children than the children can possibly give. Oprah Winfrey once interviewed several youngsters, ages twelve to sixteen, who desperately wanted babies. Several of the girls, including the twelve year old, were pregnant. Most of them had a history of sexual abuse. "It would be neat to have a baby to take care of," one said. Another admitted, "I just want someone to love me."

These young women have unrealistic expectations of themselves and of the children they will eventually bear. They are expecting the children to meet their needs and are not being realistic about the many demands children make on the parents.

The Difficult Child

Children who are physically or mentally impaired or are seen by the parent as unlovable are sometimes called high-risk children. That is, they are more likely to be abused than children who are easier to care for. When a parent's hopes for a perfectly formed child are disappointed by a birth defect or illness, the child may be seen as a disappointment and a burden. Having a baby with physical or emotional problems can be a great shock, and rearing that child can be extremely difficult. Most families are able to work through their initial grief and go on to provide excellent care. Unfortunately in some cases, the problems associated with difficult children are not resolved, and the children suffer. (Later in the book I'll go into more detail on difficult-to-manage children and what we can do to help them.)

It takes more than basic parenting skills to care for high-risk kids. If you are the parent of such a child, you need to have a strong and large support system, perhaps a support group—a place where you can openly share ideas and express your concerns and feelings.

Too Much Stress

Six-month-old Devin squirmed and wriggled as Ellen tried to diaper him. She was late for work and Devin was not cooperating. In frustration she slapped his bottom. When that didn't work, she hit him again and again.

Ellen doesn't mean to hurt her children. She loves them. But they have become an increasing burden to her. Ellen has been under a great deal of stress since her divorce from Bob. Bob's irregular child support checks forced her to take a job outside the home. Stress grew. With the burden of finding and learning a new job, she has become increasingly short-tempered. Anger at Bob and stress at work result in inappropriate behavior toward her children.

Many parents who have recently divorced, are entering the job market, or are facing financial disaster often take out their frustrations on their children. Stressful circumstances such as unemployment, divorce, moving, having a new baby, or losing a loved one have an impact on how we relate to others. Along with the stress comes an increasing inability to handle it. A crying, uncooperative child, one who has a medical problem or a disability of some sort, or one who balks at potty training may be the proverbial straw that breaks the camel's back. When stressed-out parents lose control, the child often suffers.

Again, much help is available. Many businesses, colleges, and community centers offer classes on stress reduction and anger management.

The Broken Parent

Many of you entered parenthood as victims. You may be determined not to make the same mistakes your parents did, but all too often you adopt their parenting model.

Dan sees himself as a good husband and father. He provides well for his family, makes all the important decisions, and disciplines firmly but fairly, like his father before him. And like his father, Dan works hard and long hours to make sure his family is well fed, clothed, and housed—too many hours. When he isn't working with clients, he's maintaining the yard or the car or some other urgent project. There is never enough time for the kids. He's tired to the bone—too tired to deal with three rambunctious children.

Dan grew up determined not to be like his father yet finds himself putting his children at the bottom of his priority list—just like his father did. He reads the same disappointments in his children's eyes, the same hurt he had in his own thirty years earlier. They are already feeling unimportant, unworthy, and unloved. Dan has some serious decisions to make.

It's possible for Dan to break the cycle, to change the script and rewrite his own version. If you struggle with past hurts and find yourself caught in a family saga of abuse and neglect, you can break the cycle and give your children and yourself a fresh start.

Parents sometimes damage their kids because they are themselves broken and have never had the experience of being loved by a nurturing, emotionally healthy adult. These parents may be hampered by any of the following:

- *Low self-esteem*—Parents who don't value themselves will find it difficult to value others—even their children.

- *The inability to deal with or appropriately express their feelings*—They have an especially difficult time with feelings of anger, jealousy, hatred, and fear.
- *The inability to love in healthy ways*—Many people today have a warped sense of what love really is. People who don't know how to love unconditionally may seriously damage their children by withholding love when the children don't meet their expectations.
- *Their indifference toward their child*—Perhaps even more damaging than love poorly expressed is a lack of love altogether. Claudia, for example, has no real interest in anything or anyone outside of herself. Perhaps this is because she is too intent on protecting the broken child within. She routinely yells at and slaps her child for interfering with her plans. There is no room in Claudia's life for a child with needs.

Parents who have been broken as children may have a difficult time relating to or even liking their children. Janet Pais in the book *Suffer the Children* writes about a pervasive problem among adults regarding their true feelings toward children. It can be described as contempt. Many adults, the author says, hold a basic "contempt for human weakness and need, in children and in adults themselves."[6]

Adult contempt leads to abuse. In psychotherapist Alice Miller's view:

> The contemptuous adult views the object of contempt indeed as an object, not as a person worthy of respect. Contempt itself thus is abusive and oppressive. Adults, often unconsciously, act toward children out of an attitude that the child is a possession properly subject to their control. Because adults have power over children, too often they use it, not for the true good of the child, but just to "show who is boss." Every act of child abuse is also an abuse of power, and every abuse of power necessarily implies contempt for the less powerful person.[7]

I've seen the theory played out time and again in abuse cases. Janet Pais points out:

Failing to understand a child's perceptions of reality, an adult may belittle feelings that flow from those perceptions.... An adult who has contempt for the needs of a child may neglect the child physically or emotionally or wound the child by failing to value the child.[8]

Do you have contempt for children? Have you fallen into any of the pitfalls I mentioned? Are you living in a danger zone?

There Is a Way Out

If you recognize yourself as a broken parent, seek help. A well-known author and lawyer, Andrew Vachss, who specializes in child abuse cases, says, "Emotional abuse of children can lead, in adulthood, to addiction, rage, a severely damaged sense of self and an inability to truly bond with others. But—if it happened to you—there is a way out: You carry the cure in your own heart."[9]

Believe in yourself but also believe in God. Know that while today you may still be reflecting the broken image of humankind, if you hold firm to God's promises, you "are being transformed into his likeness with ever increasing glory" (2 Cor. 3:18).

While you seek help from family, friends, and counselors, remember to seek help from God. I have seen him turn even the most impossible situations around.

Parenting is full of pitfalls but it is also full of pleasures. And one of the greatest pleasures is nurturing children. Are you the nurturer your children need?

5

THE NURTURING PARENT

Jonathan, my five-year-old grandson, recently vented his anger by saying, "I'm so mad I could exaggerate." (He loves using big words.) I chuckled and added it to my list of cute things my grandchildren say and do.

As I began to write this chapter, Jonathan's statement niggled at my mind. "I'm so mad I could exaggerate." Eventually I realized it wasn't what he said that kept drawing me back to it but the way my daughter beamed when she told me the story.

A Portrait of Excellence

My daughter, Caryl, and her husband, Ben, have four children. As I watch them care for Corisa (9), Hannah (7), Jonathan (5), and Christian (3), I am amazed. Despite the tremendous responsibilities involved in caring for four children, they are, for the most part, excellent parents.

Do they ever yell at their kids? Yes.

Are they ever exasperated? Yes.

Do they ever feel inadequate? Yes.

Do the kids ever misbehave? Yes.

Do Ben and Caryl ever make mistakes in the way they parent their children? Yes.

Perhaps you're wondering how I can give them such high marks when they have so many flaws. The answer is simple. Their high ranking as parents has nothing to do with being perfect—it has everything to do with love. Their children feel loved, valued, and safe. Each child knows he or she is important and special.

In this chapter I'd like to share two basic characteristics that I believe are essentials of good parenting. Children need parents who *nurture* them and they need parents who can *respond empathically* to their needs.

Nurture

Close your eyes and say the word *nurture*. What kind of image comes to mind? I think of a mother rocking her baby and singing a lullaby. To nurture is to care for, parent, sustain, rear, advance, cultivate, protect, develop, and train. Jesus purely reflects this characteristic. We see the nurturer in Jesus as he trained his disciples and in the way he healed the sick. We see further evidence in his lament for Jerusalem, "How often I have longed to gather your children together, as a hen gathers her chicks under her wings" (Luke 13:34).

We are all meant to have this Christ-like compassion, love, and ability to nurture. Sadly in our society, nurturing is often considered a feminine attribute—an ethereal, motherly thing. This couldn't be further from the truth. It is not a feminine trait, but a human trait.

I wrote an article for *Christian Parenting Today* called "Daddy's Turn" in which I talked about the longing in one father's heart to be more involved in his children's care.

"Isn't she the most beautiful baby in the world?" Joy, pride, and wonder fill Ken as he holds his infant daughter for the first time. His father heart bursts with love. He longs to protect her, care for her, nurture her. He wants to do more than provide a pay check and help out. He wants to be part of her life.

But he has no idea how.[1]

Most dads want to be involved in caring for their children, but, like Ken, they often waver in uncertainty. Like so many men, Ken's nurturing instincts were never encouraged; his fathering instincts never explored.

Assess Your Nurturing Skills

Whether you are a man or woman, nurturing is essential to good parenting. In appendix 1 you'll find a questionnaire to help you rate your nurturing skills. This is not a test, which you pass or fail, nor is it meant to judge you or deem you an unsuitable parent. No matter how low your evaluation might be, remember, you are not a failure. Try to see yourself as a student who simply has more to learn or as an apprentice who needs more training. Since no one needs to see the results but you, try to answer each question as honestly and objectively as possible.

How did you do? Were you surprised by the questions? These are only a sampling of the hundreds of questions we could ask ourselves. You probably noticed that nurturing deals with the practical side of child rearing. Did you find areas where you excelled? Good. Write those strengths down. Did you find areas where you need improvement? Note those as well. Remember, the assessment is not meant to intimidate or make you feel inadequate, but it is intended to help you find those areas in which you may need improvement.

Kids need nurturing parents who are able to see the needs of children, then do whatever is necessary to meet those needs. Although nurturing is instinctual in all of us, it must be enabled, encouraged, and directed. If you are not already a nurturer, perhaps by the time you've finished this book, you will have gained some of the skills to become one.

Empathy

A child in need will bring about a certain response from an adult. How the adult responds will depend on his or her background, understanding, education, and present circumstances. What the adult does in response to the need of the child will vary greatly, but the action will likely come out of one or more of these three basic reactions.[2]

1. Projection. This is when the adult projects his or her own unacceptable feelings or negative past experiences onto the child. For example, the baby is crying; she needs food. Of course, the baby has no ulterior motives, yet Mom is upset and thinks the baby is trying to make her life miserable. In a sense, the child, who simply wants her need met, becomes the bad child, who seeks to destroy the adult's happiness.

In one case, Mary felt threatened by the way her baby looked at her. The child's eyes were much like Mary's mother's eyes. In her baby's innocent eyes, Mary saw the same criticism and condemnation that she had often seen in her mother's eyes. The child suffered rejection and beatings because of Mary's projections.

2. Role reversal. In role reversal the adult uses a child as a substitute for an important adult figure who was missing from his or her own childhood. Children are expected to meet the adult's needs by filling the role of the missing individual. This is often true in child-battering cases. "Children exist only to satisfy the parent's needs and it is always the failure of the child as parent to give love which triggers the actual battering."[3]

As one young mother, Jean, said, "I never felt loved. I thought with a baby it would be different—at last I would have someone who would love me. But he kept crying and crying. He didn't love me. He wouldn't quit crying so I hit him."

We often see role reversal in high-need parents whose children learn early on to comfort their parent and strive to meet that parent's needs. It's as though they realize at an early age that the only way they can survive is to try to make that parent happy.

A few years ago I interviewed Megan, a charming, intelligent six year old, who was having anxiety attacks at school. After talking with Megan and her parents, I discovered several interesting facts. Megan often "took care" of Mommy by helping with chores and cooking. Several sessions later, Megan said, "I don't like to be in school. I'm afraid Mommy might need me during the day. When I'm gone and Daddy's gone, she doesn't have anyone to take care of her." The mother had unknowingly reversed roles with the child.

In another scenario, role reversal resulted in incest. When his wife died, Bill became increasingly dependent on his twelve-year-old daughter, Misty. Misty became the homemaker, Bill's partner, someone to talk with, watch television with, and eventually to have sex with.

Projection and role reversal are subjective responses. The child's needs are enmeshed with the adult's. These adults rarely mean to abuse. They are only trying to get their own needs met through the child. When needy adults look at their children, they may feel resentment and self-pity. They may have a kind of why-are-you-doing-this-to-me? attitude. Where you see consistent patterns of projection and reversal, you are likely to see child abuse and neglect. Abuse often comes at a point of crisis. People who abuse can be so blinded by their own needs they fail to see or perceive the needs of their children.

Parents who have suffered abuse in childhood may find it difficult to relate to their children in healthy ways. In their book *Child Abuse* Ruth S. and C. Henry Kempe write:

> For the abusive or neglectful mother, such responsiveness is not possible. Her experience has taught her that babies have no needs beyond the minimum for survival (and some mothers have a disastrously inadequate idea of what minimum is). Anything beyond that is spoiling and will result in a willful, whining child who will grow up to defy her and be nothing but trouble. When her baby cries because he is hungry or needs comforting, she misinterprets it as the beginning of the bad behavior she dreads. Oblivious to the emaciated state he reaches, she sees not a starving, helpless

infant, but some monstrously greedy parasite who will exhaust her reserves of food, energy, and love.[4]

Though many of these parents may seem well-adjusted in other ways, they often "project onto [their babies] the accumulated un-fulfilled wishes of a lifetime—a greed for love and care so great that it is frightening and cannot be tolerated lest [they] be totally engulfed."[5]

For needy parents to discuss, understand, and validate their children's needs, they must have at least some of their own needs met.

3. Empathy. There is yet another response to the needs of a child—a healthy response. Healthy parents can relax with their children and are sensitive to their children's needs. They recognize a child's needs for food, clothing, and shelter, as well as the needs for stimulation, attention, and love. When parents respond to these needs, the baby interacts with them and a mutual and satisfying bond develops.

When mature, emotionally healthy adults respond to children, they are able to empathize with or "feel" that child's need, to un-derstand, identify, and meet that need. The adult is then able to maintain enough distance from the situation to appropriately deal with it. Healthy adults listen to, act toward, and react to chil-dren with integrity.

An empathic response demands a certain objectivity in which parents can separate their own needs from the child's. No adult will always be completely empathic, but wise parents will strive to see things from their child's point of view, recognize their mis-takes as parents, and seek to rectify those mistakes.

Again, evaluate yourself. Where do you fit in the previous sce-narios? If you see some of the unhealthy characteristics of the needy parent in yourself, don't be alarmed. As I said before, it doesn't mean you're a failure as a parent or caregiver. It only means you may need training and perhaps some counseling.

Are you the kind of parent or caregiver your child needs? You may not feel you have reached that point yet, but as we move through the various ways we can put our broken children back together again, I'm certain your skills will improve and your confidence will grow.

Some of you may be struggling now with childhood wounds. Reading a book like this can be difficult because it may remind you of painful experiences you'd just as soon forget. Since this is a book for putting broken children together again, I won't be going into too much detail about how you as an adult can find healing. I do hope, however, that as you learn how to better care for your children, you will find some tools to help you nurture and care for the child in you. (If you feel broken, you may want to pick up a copy of my book *The Humpty Dumpty Syndrome: Putting Yourself Back Together Again*. It is, as my granddaughter Hannah says, "for people who are all cracked up.")

Part Three

CARING FOR BROKEN CHILDREN

Parenthood is a partnership with God.... You are working with the Creator of the universe in shaping human character and determining destiny.

Ruth Vaughn

6

DO YOU KNOW HOW CHILDREN GROW?

At sixteen, when I wanted to drive a car, I had to take a class and pass a test to prove I could adequately handle the responsibility. Before I went to work in an office, I took classes in accounting and secretarial skills. To become a nurse, and later, a counselor, I enrolled in specialized courses and attended graduate school.

The most important job I've ever had was being a parent, caring for and nurturing my children. Yet to become a parent, all I had to do was get pregnant. My self-directed training consisted of reading a few parenting books and learning by trial and error. Thankfully I had come from a loving family and had many good role models to help me muddle through.

Later as I trained to become a nurse and, more recently, a counselor, I discovered some vital information I wish I'd had when my children were younger. If we are to facilitate healing in broken children, we must be knowledgeable about how our Jacks and Jills grow. We must also understand what can happen when the growing process is hindered.

In this chapter we will be discussing the stages of growth and development, based primarily on Eric Erickson's psychosocial stages of life. According to author and psychologist Gerald Corey, "Erickson's theory of development holds that psychosexual growth and psychosocial growth take place together, and that at each stage of life we face the task of establishing an equilibrium between ourselves and our social world."[1]

The five developmental stages or tasks from infancy through adolescence are built on one another and, while listed separately, are actually interwoven.

Stage One: Infancy

Developmental task: trust versus distrust (first year of life to about eighteen months)

The first stage of a child's life involves being or becoming, learning what it is like to be alive. A baby calls out, usually by crying, when he has a need. His needs are basic—love, touch, social interaction and stimulation, adequate rest, food, cleanliness, shelter, warmth, and safety. How those needs are met determines whether or not he is able to accomplish his first developmental task—learning how to trust and in whom to place that trust. He will learn to trust if his needs are met by warm, loving, consistent, affectionate, nurturing adults who keep him safe.

In their book *Growing Up Again,* Jean Illsley and Connie Dawson suggest that in the first six months a child decides to be, to live, to thrive, to trust, to call out, to have needs met, to expect to have needs met, and to be joyful. These decisions are important to nourish and amplify throughout our lives.[2]

To children who do not learn to trust, or who misplace or misdirect their trust, the world becomes a fearful and unsafe place. They develop distrust, particularly in the area of interpersonal relationships. Trust will allow a child to explore. If he has learned to trust, he will feel safe in reaching out to touch the world. With love and adequate nurturing he will be better equipped to successfully navigate and cope with future stages of life and with developmental crises.

Stage Two: Early Childhood

Developmental task: autonomy versus shame and doubt (toddler—from about one to three years)

In this stage we see children asserting themselves, becoming separate from their parents, and having independent control over their actions. They test limits, push boundaries, and are learning to think for themselves. This is a critical time of development because so much can go wrong.

For example, Alysa's parents spank her when she wets her pants. They yell at her when she spills milk, and now that she is two, they expect her to act like a big girl. They used to hit her every time she argued with or said no to them. Now she doesn't say it anymore, at least not out loud. When she was taking a bath the other night she touched her vagina. Her mother slapped her hand away and called her a bad girl.

Alysa will probably grow up feeling ashamed and critical of herself and others. Shame may drive her to become an overachiever or to feel overly responsible. In addition, she may have trouble establishing healthy boundaries, knowing when to say no to food, drugs, inappropriate sex, and any number of things that could be harmful to her. She may struggle with her sexuality and body image. She may be afraid to take the risks that would allow her to explore her world and discover who she really is.

At this stage children need to experiment, make mistakes, and test limits within a safe environment. Psychoanalyst Eric Erickson theorized that when parents promote dependency in a child, they inhibit the child's autonomy and hamper her capacity to deal with the world successfully. Gerald Corey, psychologist and author, agrees:

> It is important at this stage that children begin to acquire a sense of their own power. If parents do too much for their children, the message transmitted is "Here, let me do thus-and-thus for you, because you are too weak or helpless to do these things for yourself." During this time children need to experiment, to make mistakes and feel that they are still acceptable persons, and to rec-

ognize some of their own power as separate and distinct individuals. So many clients are in counseling precisely because they
have lost touch with their potential for power; they are struggling
to define who they are and what they are capable of doing.[3]

Children need permission to make mistakes and to learn that
all people(even adults) err at times. Mistakes can usually be fixed.
Children must learn to apologize, clean up their messes, and get
on with life.

Stage Three: Preschool

*Developmental task: initiative versus guilt (from about three to
six years)*
In this stage of development, the healthy child achieves a sense
of competence and learns to initiate action over his environment
and to overcome feelings of powerlessness. He is aware of his body
and sexual differences and he begins to discover his role and his
level of power in relationships with adults and peers.
Erickson suggests that if children are allowed to select activities
that are personal and meaningful to them, they tend to develop a
positive view of themselves and follow through with their projects.
Not being allowed to make their own decisions or to take the initiative can produce guilt. Then, rather than taking an active stance,
they may become passive, allowing others to make decisions and
choices for them.[4]

Stage Four: School Age

Developmental task: industry versus inferiority (six to twelve years)
Industry in this stage refers to the ability to set and attain personal goals. Failure to successfully navigate this task can lead to
inferiority or a sense of inadequacy. In this stage the child's understanding of the world expands. She continues to develop an

appropriate sexual identity and learns basic skills that will help her succeed in school and in other social situations.

As one woman noted of this time in her life, "I probably didn't think of myself as stupid the first two years of school. But after six moves in those first two years—the confusion of new teachers, new routines, new faces—the inadequacy sprouted."

Corey lists several emotional problems thought to originate during middle childhood:

- a negative self-concept
- feelings of inadequacy related to learning
- feelings of inferiority in establishing social relationships
- conflict over values
- a confused sex-role identity
- unwillingness to face new challenges
- a lack of initiative
- dependency[5]

Stage Five: Adolescence

Developmental task: identity versus role confusion (twelve to eighteen years)

Adolescence is a time of transition. Once again, as for toddlers, it is a time to test limits. To establish a new adult identity, dependent ties must be broken. Parents and adolescents experience conflict as the child tries to clarify his identity and life goals, determine the meaning of life, and discover where he fits into that life. Failure to achieve a sense of identity can lead to role confusion.

The adolescent has the task of integrating a system of values that will give his life direction. In the formation of a personal philosophy of life, he must make key decisions relating to religious beliefs, sexual ethics, values, and so forth. In this search for identity, role models are especially important.[6]

As we've seen, accomplishing the developmental tasks at each stage is vital to a child's emotional well-being. How well children accomplish them will determine how well they are able to cope with difficult situations, trauma, or crises at all stages of life.

Growth and Development of the Soul

A developmental factor that is sadly missing from most of the charts is the growth and development of the soul. Children seem to be born with a strong spiritual awareness. But then didn't God promise to write the Law—the truth of his being—on our hearts? (See Jeremiah 1:5; 31:33; Romans 2:15; and Hebrews 8:10.) To illustrate, here's a child who carries a picture of God in her heart.

"What are you making?" her mother asked.

"I'm drawing a picture of God," Sarah replied.

Her mother smiled. "But no one knows what God looks like."

Sarah gave her mother a knowing smile and said, "They will when I'm done drawing him."

Scripture clearly says that we are responsible for the spiritual training of our children. "All your children shall be taught by the LORD, and great shall be the peace of your children" (Isa. 54:13 NKJV). Yet many children are denied the spiritual food needed to nourish and maintain healthy souls. Their need for spiritual growth and development is often ignored and no religious instruction is given. Or they may be given spiritual food that has been spoiled by adults who have added corrupt and poisonous elements. As a result, their souls are undernourished, and they grow up feeling incomplete. The first condition is spiritual deprivation; the second, spiritual abuse.

Spiritual Deprivation

Many children today suffer from spiritual deprivation. In an effort to separate church and state, our schools may be robbing children of moral and spiritual development. In Matthew 19:14

Jesus said, "Let the little children come to Me, and do not forbid them; for of such is the kingdom of heaven" (NKJV).

In another passage, Mark 9:42, he cautions, "And whoever causes one of these little ones who believe in Me to stumble, it would be better for him if a millstone were hung around his neck, and he were thrown into the sea" (NKJV).

When we deny our children their right—actually their *need*—for spiritual development, we violate not only a child's constitutional right to religious instruction, but the Word of God.

Spiritual Abuse

Perhaps even greater damage is done to the soul when we fill the spirit of a child with a false image of God. Authors David Johnson and Jeff VanVonderen in their excellent book *The Subtle Power of Spiritual Abuse* say:

> Churches are meant to be safe places where spiritual leaders help and equip the members for the work of service. There are some churches, however, where leaders use their spiritual authority to control and dominate others, attempting to meet their own needs for importance, power, intimacy, or spiritual gratification. Through the subtle use of the right "spiritual" words, church members are manipulated or shamed into certain behaviors or performance that ensnare them in legalism, guilt and begrudging service.
>
> This is *spiritual abuse* and the results can be shattering. Deeply ingrained spiritual codes of written and unwritten rules control and condemn, wounding believers' spirits and keeping them from the grace and joy of God's kingdom. Believers find themselves enslaved to a system, a leader, a standard of performance that saps true spiritual life.[7]

Sadly, some so-called spiritual leaders in the church and in the home lead children to believe not in the true God, but in an angry, controlling, stern, unbending tyrant. Hannah Whitall Smith in her work *The God of All Comfort* says:

I rejoice to tell you: The stern Judge is not there. He does not exist!

The God who does exist is the God and Father of our Lord Jesus Christ, the God who so loved the world that He sent His Son, not to judge the world but to save it (John 3:16–17). He is the God who anointed Jesus Christ to bind up the brokenhearted, and to proclaim liberty to captives, and to comfort all that mourn . . . (Luke 4:18).

Throughout His life on earth, Jesus fulfilled this divine mission. When His disciples asked Him to call down fire from heaven to consume some people who refused to receive Him, Jesus turned and rebuked them: "You do not know what kind of spirit you are of, for the Son of Man did not come to destroy lives, but to save them" (Luke 9:55).[8]

It's no wonder we find so many adults and children today looking for their missing part. The child in them may still be trying to draw a picture of God, but their broken adult selves deny and reject the true image, selecting instead the one distorted by human experience. The false image leaves them disillusioned and empty. Some turn away insisting they no longer have need of spiritual things. Others attempt to feed their spirits with friends, work, money, power, drugs, alcohol, sex, or food. And still they come up empty.

Unless the spirit of each child is nurtured and developed and unless his or her social and moral conscience is cultivated, we will continue to produce thieves, rapists, and murderers. Psychoanalyst Eric Erickson has said:

> Someday, maybe there will exist a well-informed, well-considered and yet fervent public conviction that the most deadly of all possible sins is the mutilation of a child's spirit; for such mutilation undercuts the life principle of trust, without which every human act, may it feel ever so good, and seem ever so right, is prone to perversion by destructive forms of consciousness.[9]

A Child's Image of God

A child's image of God directly corresponds to the image of those who are in authority over him. All too often, that is a false image and it does not match the image of the God who resides in the child's heart. The results can be devastating to a child's spiritual development. Instead of peace and joy he finds shame, confusion, misplaced loyalty, and paranoia.

Our task in helping children grow will be to present them with a Christ-like role model. As we encourage our children to successfully grow and develop through each phase of their lives, we will want to be especially careful to include healthy spiritual training.

Someone to Love Them

Children who have been severely broken—physically, sexually, emotionally, or spiritually—who have been abused over a long period of time, who have not been allowed to accomplish their developmental tasks—especially those of trust and autonomy—will probably need much time and attention and, in some cases, intense counseling to get well. Some may not recover until they are adults and some may not recover at all. Much depends on whether or not traumatized children have someone to nurture and care for them—to help them deal with the abuse and give them a reason to heal.

Dawn was eight years old when her father sexually assaulted her. Instead of embracing and offering comfort, her mother angrily accused her of causing the problem. For years Dawn carried the shame and blame of the incestuous act. It happened only once, but the trauma has lasted a lifetime.

Had her mother taken Dawn's side, been her advocate, loved her, and assured her that she was a victim, not the initiator, the trauma might have been lessened. Dawn had no one to protect her and sympathize with her, no one to hold her and give her the hope that everything would be all right, and no one to give her a reason to trust again.

Every child needs an advocate, a champion—someone to walk alongside her, protect her, and love her. That person can help restore, reclaim, and preserve the wonder of childhood.

7

RECLAIMING THE WONDER
OF CHILDHOOD

One day while Corisa, then three, and I were playing in the park, I gave her a push on the swing. I couldn't help noticing the look of sheer delight on her face. Wondering what was going on in her head, I asked, "What's swinging like?"

She tipped her head back and thought for a moment, then replied, "Nanna, it's like a summer day."

Have you ever taken time to experience the imagination of a child? There is something fresh and innocent and almost magical about children—especially when you are a grandparent. I am continually amazed at their innate sense of wisdom and wonder.

The Wonder of It All

My friend Gail recently shared a story about her daughter, Marla, as a small child. Gail and her husband were driving home one night when they heard an alarmed cry from the backseat. "Oh, no! Look! The moon is broken." The adults looked up to where the tiny finger pointed. There in the night sky hung a narrow sliver of a moon, where only a few days ago it had been whole.

Before they could explain about moon shadows, Marla sighed and said, "Oh well, that's all right. My daddy will fix it." In a child's mind anything can happen. A daddy can even fix the moon.

Several years ago, Corisa, then age four, and I were philosophizing about life. She began to tell me about her "people of the eye."

"What do you mean?" I asked.

She looked at me as though this were a piece of wisdom everyone should know, then realizing I was just an adult, explained it to me. "People of the eye are ones you love that have to go away. But even if they're gone you can still see them when you close your eyes. Those are people of the eye."

"Wow," I said, "did you think of that all by yourself?"

"Yes." She nodded and grinned. "I also thought about people of the nose."

As you can imagine, the conversation went downhill from there.

Where do these wild, wonderful, imaginative, and at times even spiritual thoughts come from? More important, where do they go when we grow older and why do so many of us leave them behind? Many theorists suggest that as people grow into adulthood and become more focused and goal-oriented, the place for wonder disappears. Our time and thoughts are then almost exclusively devoted to the routine and mundane.

When we somehow cause children to lose their sense of wonder and childlikeness, when we keep them from fulfilling their developmental tasks, we are inflicting damage that takes its toll in their ability to cope, to trust, and to become self-confident, healthy adults.

Think for a moment of your own life and the childlike qualities you may have lost on the way to adulthood. We all have to grow up, but I don't think God actually meant for us to lose so many pieces of ourselves along the way. If that were the case, why would Jesus tell us that in order to gain eternal life we'd need to become like children? We'd have to regain those precious qualities that were somehow lost to us. For that reason, one of our primary goals in working with broken children will be to preserve or reclaim their childlike ways—their sense of wonder and ability to trust, their resilience, honesty, transparency, loving nature, and holiness.

Trust

Children who trust the adults in their lives respond to them with utter abandon. The other day I watched as a dad set his son, who was about three, on a high platform. The little boy lifted his arms and threw himself into his daddy's arms. He had no fear and no doubt that Dad would catch him.

Children don't generally worry about who will care for them, where they will live, or what they will eat, drink, and wear. But experience with people who don't catch them or care for them or meet their needs teaches distrust.

A teacher comments, "I've seen young parents wait until the last minute to catch a child. These parents seem to get a thrill out of the anxiety they cause the children. One parent even said, 'I don't want her to trust anyone too deeply. She'll get hurt.' This mother's warped sense of protection made her miss the point of trust and how easily it can be destroyed."

In an excellent article on emotional abuse, Andrew Vachss stated, "We must renounce the lie that emotional abuse is good for children because it prepares them for a hard life in a tough world. I've met some individuals who were prepared for a hard life that way— I met them while they were *doing* life."[1]

To maintain a sense of trust, children need to feel safe and nurtured. We must meet their needs. Trust, of course, is the first of our developmental tasks. It is the foundation on which we build our lives and relationships and it affects every part of our being—the physical, emotional, and spiritual.

Children tend to believe until experience gives them reason not to. In a child's mind anything is possible—even the wisdom of grandmothers. One day Corisa and I were having one of our philosophical discussions. Not yet having discovered my intellectual shortcomings, she said, "Nanna, you know everything."

I smiled (naturally), "Thank you for thinking that, honey, but only God knows everything."

She thought for a moment and, in a tone that brooked no opposition, said, "No, Nanna. You and God know everything."

When I shared the story with a friend, she responded by saying, "For Corisa this is probably true. You know everything she *needs* to know to be secure, comfortable, and happy at this time in her life."

Although they may not always be entirely accurate, children can often grasp certain concepts adults can't fathom. Many adults, for example, have difficulty with the concept of a Triune God— the Father, Son, and Holy Spirit. As adults we may have an intellectual knowledge of the Trinity but do we really experience it in the sense of knowing? Children often do.

My daughter and her husband recently moved to Minnesota from Washington State. For several months before the actual move, her husband worked in Minnesota. At one point he brought home a video showing the home he'd found for them. When Hannah, who was two, saw her daddy in the video, she insisted there were two daddies. The one on television was still in Minnesota and the other was sitting with her in the living room. He was the same daddy in two parts.

Our rational, adult minds might say, "That's nonsense." Certainly our intellect has progressed to the point where there is no mystery in Hannah's two-daddy theory. But have we, in gaining what we call reason, also lost the ability to believe in the unreasonable? For a child, all things are possible, even the virgin birth or the concept of God in us, until logic, reason, and unbelief desecrate the miraculous.

Part of our responsibility in caring for children is to encourage them to explore possibilities and hold dear the element of mystery.

Resilience

Even severely abused children, when given over to loving, caring parents, can go on to live healthy, productive lives. Children are like soft, pliant clay that the Master Potter has loaned us to shape. For a time they are resilient, unassuming, and naturally forgiving. We shape their values and make impressions on their lives.

If we are not nurturing enough, if their needs are not sufficiently met, if they are too often treated cruelly or with contempt, they will put up defenses that will eventually cause them to harden. As children become increasingly damaged, they become more rigid, afraid to take chances, afraid to bend.

Unfortunately, once a child hardens, it's extremely difficult to bring him back. He may become inflexible and unwilling to trust, and our attempts to influence him can be like trying to carve our initials into stone.

Sometimes it's possible, sometimes not. Hardness of heart and loss of trust, hope, and resilience present one of our greatest challenges in caring for wounded children. Yet love, the presence of God in our lives, and belief in a child's ability to overcome the past, can soften even the hardest of hearts.

While discussing this book with my friend Margo, she commented, "We don't give kids enough credit. They can take a lot more than we might imagine. I think one of the biggest mistakes we can make is to assume their lives are going to be ruined because someone abused them."

I agree. We need to reinforce what they already sense, that God has equipped them with fierce inner strength to handle suffering and adversity and that by tapping into it, they can make it through anything.

Honesty

Have you ever noticed how blatantly honest children can be? Gene, father of three, was speeding on the way to a family outing. Red lights flashing in his rearview mirror directed him to pull over. Gene swore and muttered, "I've got a good notion to give that jerk a piece of my mind."

When the police officer approached the car, Gene rolled down the window and smiled. "Hello officer, what's the trouble?"

"Hey, Dad," his son Ron piped up from the backseat. "Aren't you gonna give that jerk a piece of your mind like you said?"

When children hurt, they cry; when they are happy, they laugh. Their emotions are as much a part of them as skin. They will express them openly and honestly—until they learn that being open is unacceptable or that telling the truth can get them into trouble. It could cause Mom and Dad to get mad, go away, and not love them anymore.

Children come into the world naked and unashamed. They learn to cover their honesty with lies, their trust with doubt, their fear with arrogance, their sorrow with anger, and their laughter with contempt.

Transparency

Closely related to honesty is transparency. Transparency is an unguarded state, devoid of egocentrism. In a seminary spirituality class, my professor, Frances Whiting, shared a story that to me beautifully illustrates the idea of transparency.

A boy and his father visited a lavish ancient cathedral. They stood transfixed by the beauty and translucence of the figures in the stained glass windows that lined the walls. "Daddy," the little boy pulled on his father's arm and whispered, "who are those people the light shines through?"

The light still shines through Kyrstin, my five-year-old granddaughter, who loves to sing, "This little light of mine, I'm gonna let it shine." She's bold and sincere and belts out the song with conviction. Light dances in her eyes and glistens in her smile as she sings and signs the song she learned in Sunday school. I hope the light in her eyes and in her heart will shine forever.

The Bible tells us to be shining lights, but, sadly, as children lose their ability to trust, the light disappears into the shadows of insecurity and fear. Our windows become stained and dull, dirtied by wrongs and covered by denial.

As parents and caregivers, we will want to encourage children to shed their dense protective layers and let their reality show through once more, but we'll need to provide a safe place for them to do this. We'll be talking more about that safe place—a place to be—in the next chapter.

A Child's Love

Angie was only six when her best friend, Laurie, was killed in an automobile accident. After the funeral, Angie walked to where her friend's mother sat, climbed onto her lap, and put her small wiry arms around the woman's neck. Love flowed from Angie to Laurie's mother. Love for that moment was a little girl who filled a grieving mother's empty arms.

A child's spontaneous, unconditional, unconscious love is hard to destroy. Even an abused child continues, at least for a time, to love. To love is a part of human nature—the image of God in us. Unfortunately many children lose their natural ability to love. Love is lost in the elaborate defense systems they create to protect themselves against those who fail to love them in appropriate ways.

Love, like a refreshing mountain stream, begins with God, flows into individuals, then out to others. If we stop the flow, love's essence changes and it may become impure, stagnant, and rancid. The love of children will flow until we teach them that they need to erect barriers.

The Nearest Thing to Heaven

You may have heard it said, "The nearest thing to heaven is a child." There are two points in life at which we are closest to God—at birth and at death. The following poem reflects that thought.

Two of a Kind
Her skin wrinkled, paper thin over blue veins;
His is six-month baby smooth, honey-colored with a rosy
  hue.

Her hands touch him lightly;
His pull her hair.
She has some bald spots.
He does, too.
She talks in words that only he can understand.
He laughs, but she can't hear.
Two of her front teeth are missing—
It doesn't matter, he hasn't *any.*
Born in eighteen eighty-four,
She has almost lived a lifetime;
He has just begun.
They sit together
spanning the century,
    each so very close
        to the Source of Life,
Two of God's children.

Nancy White Carlstrom

At birth we come into a world tainted with evil and disease. As children travel through life, they are drawn toward or pulled away from the Source of Life. Certain experiences may prompt them to make wrong choices, taking them further and further away from God. Children lose their childlikeness—their integrity. They begin to dis-integrate. They become broken. Many children will not regain what they have lost unless someone comes along to take their hands and lead them back. That is our job.

To do that job well, we may need to reclaim our own losses. We may need to take Jesus' advice and "become as little children" so that we can better understand the losses of children and help them deal with the pain.

How do we become childlike? The New World dictionary defines childlike as "characteristics typical of a child . . . suggesting favorable qualities such as innocence, guilelessness, trustfulness."

Becoming childlike doesn't mean being childish. It simply means taking back these wondrous God-given gifts we may have lost while growing up:

- *Sense of wonder.* Let yourself experience awe in nature, in children, and in God.

- *Ability to trust and believe.* We can't always trust people but we can trust God. He is the parent who will never leave or forsake us. Believe in your child, in yourself, and in the power of God to accomplish good things in all of us.

- *Resilience.* Adopt a flexible attitude. Let God mold and shape you into the parent he'd like you to be.

- *Openness and honesty.* Develop a healthy appreciation for being real in the way you express your thoughts and feelings. Your openness fosters openness in others.

- *Transparency.* Let your light shine. Let your child see the love and compassion of God in you.

- *Ability to love.* Unconditional love is the cornerstone of successful parenting. Love may not always change behaviors or circumstances but it does provide a safe environment where children can be who they really are.

- *Spirituality.* Get close to the Source of Life. Let God renew the spiritual openness of the child in you. Develop the spiritual part of your self and strive for wholeness (holiness), so that you can in turn pass your wholeness on to the children in your care.

As childlike adults we can more fully appreciate children and their ways. As we embrace the child within us—the child we used to be—we gain a new perspective and can more fully value the children in our homes and communities. In becoming childlike, we shed some of our adult defenses and coverings such as denial, indifference, and resignation. With renewed empathy and compassion we can more confidently offer help and healing to the Jacks and Jills who have been broken.

Am I saying that we can somehow create a perfect world for children where they will never have to suffer? No. We all know that's not possible. Everyone suffers a certain amount of loss through life. As M. Scott Peck so simply states, "Life is difficult."

We are imperfect people living in an imperfect world. We make mistakes. We fall and we break. But, as caretakers of children, we can do something to diminish and, in some cases, even end the brokenness. We can offer comfort, protection, and encouragement. We can make the falls less traumatic and we can provide survival tools so that the children can move on.

8

A Place to Be

You may remember a widely broadcast story about a little boy who filed for a divorce from his natural parents. According to the news coverage, his mother and father had abused and abandoned him. He was eventually taken in by foster parents who loved him and wanted to adopt him.

He stole our hearts when he asked the judge for one thing: "I just want a place to be." This was a simple request—something every child should have. That little boy echoed the heart cry of every broken child in today's world.

A few years ago a good friend was working as a counselor for an organization that helped urban teenagers. Many of the kids she counseled were gang members. She attributed much of their participation in gangs to their need for a place to be. They often joined gangs because they needed to be where people recognized them and called them by name, where they were accepted unconditionally and made to feel a part of the group.

Everyone needs to feel important and worthwhile, and kids will often go to extremes to find their place to be. When they don't find acceptance, or they feel worthless and unloved, they may search for some kind of worth within themselves. Some try to earn acceptance by being the best player on the team, by getting the best grades, or by having perfect bodies.

We live in a world where Barbie look-alikes, with their slender figures, youthful skin, peaches-and-cream complexions, and long, gorgeous hair have become the coveted ideal for young women. How can a young woman feel valued when she realizes she doesn't fit the mold? What happens when she learns that her face and figure aren't good enough to appear in *Glamour* magazine?

In an effort to stay slim and beautiful, girls begin to worry about their figures and may start dieting as early as age seven. It's no wonder so many fall prey to eating disorders and paranoia about their weight.

Boys also struggle with achieving the right image. A television news program recently featured a young man who felt he needed to excel in sports to feel that he was of value. He began taking steroids so he could compete with the strongest and best. Steroids, as we know, have side effects—one of those being what we might term temper tantrums. One night in a fit of rage he killed his girlfriend and is now in prison.

We ask ourselves why? Who's to blame? What would drive a child to take such a damaging drug? Often children choose dangerous paths because they feel that they don't matter. They do not feel valued as they are.

Too many kids today grow up with an unhealthy obsession with clothes, perfect bodies, sports, good grades, and the like. They have been made to feel that these are what are important, and when they don't measure up, they may try to ease the pain of inadequacy and low self-esteem with drugs, alcohol, food, and sexual promiscuity. Some even turn to suicide.

A Family

Kids need a family—a community of people who truly care for them and give them a place to be. All children need to feel as though they belong, that they have a purpose and a place. We can meet that need in our children by providing an environment in which they feel appreciated just as they are and in which they are players with a significant role.

I was fortunate to be raised in that kind of warm, caring environment. I grew up in a small farming community in the Midwest. My father had come to the United States from Sweden and met my mother, a Norwegian, in North Dakota. Mom was one of thirteen children from the Olsen clan.

My parents, grandparents, aunts, and uncles adored me. Two uncles, especially, used to come in every day from working in the fields or milking cows and play with me before supper. I remember my grandparents most of all. Since my father was gone a great deal—first in the service, then in a sanitarium with tuberculosis—my mother and I stayed with Mum and Papa (my grandparents). I used to crawl into their bed and snuggle between them on frosty mornings. They always had a smile and a hug for me. I can never remember a time when I felt that I didn't belong.

We were a close-knit family, and the entire clan gathered at my grandparents' home to celebrate birthdays, anniversaries, holidays, and Sundays. Every year at Christmas we drew names and exchanged gifts. I don't remember much about the presents but I do remember the laughter, the warmth, and the food. We were a family, a wheel of endless love. Caring relatives, like spokes, reached out from the hub. My grandparents were at the center and God was the axle that made it turn.

I'm sure no one in my family ever really stopped to think about the psychological impact he or she was having on my life. We didn't worry much in those days about co-dependency, dysfunction, and recovery. We just followed the golden rule: "Do unto others as you would have them do unto you." And we tried to follow the Lord's commands, "Love God," and "Love one another." My family lived out the philosophy of "Children are for loving, not for hurting" in their consistent communal love and support.

"How did Grandpa and Grandma keep thirteen children in line?" I asked my mother the other day. "Did you get a lot of spankings?"

"No. They didn't give many spankings. I only remember a couple of times when Dad spanked two of the boys."

"A couple? With thirteen kids?"

"I guess we just knew what we needed to do."

"With that many children, how did your mom and dad give each child the attention he or she needed?"

"I'm not sure. I know we spent a lot of time together. I remember Dad bringing out his guitar after supper almost every night and we'd gather around him and sing songs. Sometimes the little ones would sit in his lap. I'm not sure how the folks managed it, but they took good care of us."

By reminiscing I don't mean to paint a picture of a utopia where nothing ever went wrong. Life was hard, particularly during the depression and World War II. If you've ever spent a winter in the Midwest or had your survival depend on the whims of Mother Nature, you know how difficult times can be. My mother's family didn't have much money. In fact some Christmases the children had little more than an orange or a hankie in their stockings. But they had something more precious than money and material things. They had each other, and if hardship did anything, it brought them closer together. Each child was needed and had a special place in the scheme of things. Everyone had jobs and worked together to maintain the farm and, later on, the house in town.

And they had faith. Their belief in God strengthened and preserved them as they worked and played and prayed together.

When I came along, it was family interaction, tradition, and faith that taught me right from wrong. I was encouraged to grow physically, intellectually, emotionally, and spiritually. When I wanted to be a ballerina, my family couldn't afford lessons so they bought me a book. When I wanted to be an artist, they gave me art supplies. They never said, "You can't be . . ."

I'm Glad You Were Born

We can give our children a "place to be" by giving verbal and nonverbal messages like the following.

- I'm excited that you were born and that you are here with me.
- You are part of our family and belong with us.
- Your needs are important to me.

- I will take care of you for as long as you need me.
- I love you and want to take care of you.
- This is a safe place where you can be yourself.
- You are free to explore, experiment, and learn, knowing that I am here to protect you.
- Here you can grow at your own pace and take as much time to learn new things as you need.
- I will respect and accept our differences. I am happy you are you and I am me.
- I'm happy that you can think for yourself.
- You are free to express your feelings and emotions here. You can be happy, sad, stubborn, angry.
- You can feel secure because I will protect you. I will not let you hurt yourself or others.
- I enjoy watching you and delight in the things you do and say.
- You can always be free to ask for help and talk about whatever you want.
- You can discover who you are and what you want to be.
- You can learn about choices and making right decisions.
- You can learn about making mistakes, suffering consequences, and becoming responsible.
- You can learn to listen to your conscience and your intuition to help you make the best choices for you.
- You can learn to solve problems and find solutions.
- I love you for being you and I love learning and growing with you.

To give a child a place to be is to hold him in high esteem, to treasure him and find value in him. Children who are not valued by others will find it almost impossible to value themselves.

"Not every culture abuses its children," an American Indian friend told me. "Traditionally Indians treasured their children and treated them with utmost respect. They had a saying that went something

like this: 'Children are gifts from the Creator. We must treat them
well, or the Creator will take them away.'"

He thought for a moment, then added, "The Indians had another saying: 'Whites treat their horses better than they treat
their children.'"

Unfortunately his second comment may be true for people of
all colors. All too often children are relegated to the lower end of
the priority list. If we have children, we must place them at the
top of the list. That's not to say we can't have a job or be involved
with other people or activities. It's saying that when it comes to
making choices, we must consider the needs of our children first.

Being Valued

It has been said, "Every child should be a wanted child." In a
sense that is true but it is also misleading. Most parents want
their children—at least for a time. But wanting a child is not the
same as treasuring or valuing a child. Many parents want children for selfish reasons. Some may want children so that a troubled marriage can be improved or the family name will be continued. Others may think a baby will make them feel good. It's
much like wanting a cat or dog or parakeet.

Treasuring a child does not mean embracing that child for the
benefits you may reap, but for the love you can share with another
human being. The treasuring must come out of your love of the
child's being, not his doing. Anything else will cause a child to feel
unworthy.

Being Valued Builds Resilience

What I learned from feeling loved and valued as a child has
played an important part in my life as an adult. I was able to develop self-value or worth, and this has given me strength and resilience. I learned how to be stoic, when necessary, which is not
always a negative thing. For me, having a little stoicism simply
means that I can reach inside myself for strength to carry on,

knowing that God will guide me through. I learned how to be unsinkable, to endure hardship, and to overcome adversity.

Being valued has also given me the courage to push the boundaries of mediocrity and fear—to risk becoming the person God created me to be. My family's love and faith gave me the ability to believe in God and in the reconciling work of Jesus Christ. The result is that I have a deep sense of peace about my place and my being.

I recently came across this quote by Gladys Hunt, author of *Family Secrets*, that sums up my feelings toward my family very well: "Looking back I realize you had a basic commitment to our childhood—you understood the nature of the child and created an environment fitting for his nurture. There was a certainty about life from which we derived an enormous sense of security."

I don't see my extended family very often these days. The aunts and uncles who are still living are grandmas and grandpas to their own broods. Sad in a way, I suppose, but life goes on. I'm a grandmother myself now, and it's up to me to see that the tradition of providing a place to be continues in my own family, with my own children and grandchildren.

Helping Children Feel Valuable

The older I become, the more impressed I am with the importance of carrying on the tradition of treasuring children. I have become a watchdog, in a sense, wanting to build into our grandchildren the same sense of value that I felt as a child. I want them to feel important to the family and thus the community as a whole. I'd like them all to know they have a place to be.

M. Scott Peck in his book *Meditations from the Road* says, "The time and quality of the time that their parents devote to them indicate to children the degree to which they are valued by their parents."[1]

To instill in our children a sense of being valued, we must first get to know our children well. We say things to them verbally and nonverbally that let them know how we feel about them, things like "I'm glad you were born and that you are a part of our family." "I enjoy being with you." "You draw clowns better than anyone I know." "You are important to me." We get to know their likes and dislikes, their concerns, fears, and passions. It is important to make eye contact with children and smile as though you think they are adorable.

Peck tells us, "The feeling of being valuable is a cornerstone of self-discipline because when you consider yourself valuable you will take care of yourself. . . . In this way self-discipline is self-caring."[2]

Children who are valued and who learn to value themselves are less likely to go along with activities or behaviors that could harm them. When adults value the children in their lives, they hold those children in high esteem. One way to do that is to imitate God and practice seeing children as God sees us. Looking at how God values us can help us see not only our children but every individual in a positive light.

Seeing People through God's Eyes

The Bible not only reveals the value God places on us, but gives us insight into our role as parents and caregivers.

In Genesis 1–3, we find the following.

- We are created in God's image. God is a part of our being just as we are part of our children's being. When I use the term "our children" I am not only referring to our biological children, but all children, for we humans are all part of the same family.
- We are created with intellect and the ability to communicate and to rule over the earth. What a wonderful inheritance to pass on to future generations.
- "And God saw all that He had made, and behold, it was very good" (1:31 NASB). Let's look at our children, ourselves, and others and see the good present in us before the fall and the good that was restored by Christ's reconciling act of redemption.
- He gives us power to make our own choices in life. The responsibility is not to be taken lightly. We must show our chil-

dren how both right and wrong choices affect us as individuals and as a community.

- Adam and Eve, wanting more power, chose evil over good. Yet even then God continued to cherish those he had created in his likeness.

In Psalm 8:3–9, we read about how God sees us.

- God thinks about us and takes care of us.
- He designed us to be "a little lower than God" (8:5 NASB).
- The Lord crowns us with glory and majesty and has put all things under our feet. We have much responsibility, power, and authority. We must show children how to access that power. Unfortunately far too many people grow up thinking they are powerless victims with no control over their lives.

Read Psalm 139 and discover that

- God knew us before we were born.
- Wherever we go, he is there.
- We are precious to him.

John 3:16 tells us:

- God loves us so much that he sent his Son to suffer and die in our place because of our sins.
- His act of love makes it possible for us to be reunited with him and restored to our former goodness.

We can be encouraged by the words of John 14:1–3, 16:

- He offers us eternal life with him in heaven.
- God sends the Holy Spirit to guide and comfort us.

Hebrews 1:14 says:

- God sends angels to watch over us.

Matthew 19:13–15 tells us how Jesus felt about children:

- When the disciples denied children access to Jesus, he admonished the adults saying: "Let the little children come to Me, and do not forbid them; for of such is the kingdom of heaven" (19:14 NKJV).
- Jesus loved and accepted children and gave them a place of honor, thereby validating their existence and giving them a place to be. When we accept and love our children we validate them and in a sense help to make them complete.

God's love and acceptance of us is unconditional. Since his love is unconditional, nothing we do or don't do can diminish it. We are loved for the simple reason that we exist. Love comes freely, with no limits, requirements, or expectations. To God we are priceless. Nothing could have kept God from doing whatever was necessary to restore our relationship with him. God knows what we need and provides a way for those needs to be met. God delights in us.

One of the most profound ways God shows us how valuable we are to him is his consistent desire to be in relationship with us. This same desire in adults is primary in parenting wounded children. We, too, must show our children how treasured they are by developing an intimate and lasting relationship with them.

9

Building Lasting Relationships

My daughter once said, "Home is a place you can come back to no matter who you are or what you've done." Over the years I've come to regard this as one of the most precious compliments I've ever received. Regardless of the mistakes I made while they were young, my children know I love them and that I would always welcome them home. I have somehow managed, with God's help, to build lasting relationships with them.

As my children were growing up, I never really thought much about developing or maintaining relationships with them. After all, we were family and we had bonded.

As they grew older, however, I could feel them slipping away. I realized I would have to work at being a parent if I wanted them to confide in and relate to me. Unfortunately I sometimes got confused about what really mattered. I tried to be available to them when they needed me, but with a job, housework, and all my other responsibilities, the children sometimes didn't get as large a slice of my time as they should have. Like so many other mothers, I had joined the supermom brigade and taken on more than I could handle.

For a time I fell into a trap of feeling inadequate because I couldn't live up to the standards I had set for myself. Devastated by failure, I went into a serious depression and checked out for a few weeks.

The bout with depression, though devastating at the time, actually turned into a blessing. Forced to slow down, I became more intimately acquainted with God, my family, and myself.

Eventually I came to my senses. I realized that to enhance the relationships within my family, I would have to be less involved in projects and more involved in them. I've learned a great deal about people and relationships since then. Although I managed to do some things right, if I could do it all again, I would change a few things. I would try to:

- be more available—in time and in attentiveness
- be a better listener in order to know and understand my children
- see parenting not only as a serious responsibility, but as an opportunity for growth
- worry less about being a great homemaker and concentrate more on being a loving mom
- worry less about what I couldn't do and feel better about the accomplishments
- concentrate more on developing moral values in my children and less on trying to please them with toys and clothes

These are all important elements in building strong, healthy relationships, and we'll be looking at them in more detail as we go on. I made mistakes as a mother. Most of us do. One of my problems stemmed from not realizing early on that relationships don't just happen.

As a young mother I did not realize how much work developing the parent/child relationship could be. I thought it just came naturally. I was wrong. While we may be born relational beings, we do not automatically relate to others in healthy or appropriate ways.

Developing a relationship with a child doesn't just happen. There is no button on the brain you can push when the time is right. No parent or caregiver should assume that because you care for a child, you automatically become a nurturer or have an intimate relationship with that child. Though you may have bonded with the infant, you can't expect that bond to stretch the span of

93

a child's life without working at it and making some necessary adjustments. Building lasting relationships with our children takes a lifetime of commitment, adjustments, persistence, planning, and, most important, love.

Love Is the Foundation

As I mentioned earlier, I made mistakes as a young parent but I also managed to do some things right. Perhaps because of my family background, I instinctively nurtured and gave unconditional love to my babies.

Love didn't come easy, however, as my children slipped into adolescence. My son was fiercely independent and strong willed, intent on going his own way. His unloving attitude and hateful words began to tear apart the fabric of my love for him. I tried to be understanding and patient, but there were times I felt like giving up and disowning him.

Some parents I knew had done just that, given up. As one father said, "What's the use? Why should I put out all this effort to love someone who doesn't love me in return?" I could empathize. His son had run away from home, gotten heavily into drugs, and then seemed to prefer living on the street to coming home.

Some damaged children in our care may be very difficult to love. We must, though, reach beyond our own needs and offer them unconditional love—a love given freely, not based on their performance. This may be impossible if we think that love is an emotional response to others rather than a deliberate act. Unconditional love is not so much something we feel or say, but something we do. When I teach writing classes, one of my most repeated statements is, "Show it; don't tell it." This is true also in the art of loving children. The words are important, but as the old cliché goes: Actions speak louder than words.

Here are some ways we show love for our children.

- We meet their needs and provide a safe environment.

- We accept each child as a different and unique person with his own special temperament, tastes, and talents. We provide a place where each child can explore and create and gain a sense of himself.
- We give our children the respect they deserve as individuals created in God's image.
- We are honest in sharing our feelings and concerns.
- We are open and do not cover up problems and pretend they don't exist. Rather, whenever possible, we bring problems into the foreground and talk about ways to deal with them.
- We show understanding and empathy for children when they make mistakes or get into trouble.
- We are patient. Children do not always grow and develop and learn at the speed we adults may expect. We must be sensitive to the need for children to learn at their own speed. Our frustration can make children feel inadequate and can impede their progress. We praise them often and expect greatness.
- We become personally involved in our children's lives, their religious activities, day care, school, sports.
- We take time to get to know each child intimately.

Relationships Take Time

I know, I know. I'm starting to sound like a broken record about this time thing, but it's so important. Having a large enough slice of a parent or guardian's time is important to a child. Sometimes it can make the difference in whether he sees himself as being loved and valued or as someone who just gets in the way. My friend Angela shared this story from her past.

"There are seven kids in my family and I'm the oldest. I had to pick up a lot of slack for my mom. Looking back, I have a hard time remembering her doing anything with me alone, except for this: Every once in a while she would take me out on a long walk. We would walk around the neighborhood for about an hour. We were alone. I don't remember her reading to me or anything in particular but I remember those walks.

"That's why it's so important for me to spend time with my kids. I saw a poem once that included this line, 'I wish I'd found the time to do the little things you asked me to.' Perhaps that's the lament of every mother. I don't know but I try to do something with them alone every day. Sometimes it's just reading with them before bed. I take walks with my kids too."

Be More Available

How often are you available to your children? Marita, a stay-at-home mom, said proudly, "All the time. I'm here when they come home from school and we're together most of the time."

Sally, a single mom who works full time as a nurse, says guiltily, "When I'm not working or sleeping. I guess that leaves evenings and a couple of days during the week. I try to make sure we have some special time together every evening and spend one day a week fooling around. We might go to the zoo, for a hike, on a picnic—that sort of thing."

While making time for kids can be difficult for parents who are working outside of the home, it need not be a major problem. Availability, after all, entails more than the hours and minutes you are together. Parents may be in the same house with their children but are not really "with" them or available to them.

Let's look at Sally and Marita, for example. Marita, it turns out, isn't as available as she thinks. With PTA, Bible study, women's ministry, various craft classes, shopping, and other homemaking duties, Marita spends nearly as much time away from home as does Sally. When Marita is at home, she is doing housework or making meals, while the kids busy themselves with television, video games, and other activities. When pressed for the number of hours she allots solely to the children, she came up with about ten per week—an average of 1.43 hours a day.

Sally logs in three times as many child/parent hours as Marita. How is that possible? Since Sally has so little time at home, she places a high value on it and keeps a schedule. She has worked at creating open times especially geared to being with her children. She has purposely scheduled in appointments with her two children singly or the two together.

In addition, Sally found she could free up as many as fifteen to twenty hours a week by limiting television time. Then she has more time for herself and for her children. Because they watch less television, they read together, play games, and talk.

How does Sally get her chores done? She doesn't always. The children come home to a part-time nanny (an older woman), who also does some light housework and bakes cookies. While waiting for Mom to come home, the kids do their homework or crafts and visit with their nanny. Even though Sally schedules in time for cleaning, shopping, and preparing meals, she isn't always able to dust and vacuum as often as she'd like, but she has her priorities. On the wall above the rocker in her bedroom is a saying her mother had embroidered and handed down. It reads:

> Cleaning and scrubbing can wait 'til tomorrow.
> For babies grow up, we've learned to our sorrow.
> So quiet down, cobwebs.
> Dust, go to sleep.
> I'm rocking my baby and babies don't keep.

By using Marita and Sally as examples, I'm not saying all moms should take jobs outside the home so they can spend more time with their children. I'm just saying we need to differentiate between being at home *for* the kids and actually being *with* them. You may want to do an accounting of how much time you really are available to your children. Try a schedule like Sally's or keep a journal for a few weeks. Log in the actual hours and minutes in a day when you are actively *with* your children.

You may find it necessary to drop certain activities and rearrange your schedule. Children, especially those who are difficult to manage or who have been traumatized by abuse and neglect, require a great deal of time, attention, and love.

Reading to your children is a good way to spend time with them. Make it a point to read every day. I came across a poem the other day written by Srickland W. Gillilan called *The Reading Mother.*

I had a mother who read to me
Sagas of pirates who scoured the sea,
Cutlasses clenched in their yellow teeth,
"Blackbirds" stowed in the hold beneath.
I had a mother who read me lays
Of ancient and gallant and golden days,
Stories of Marmion and Ivanhoe,
Which every boy has a right to know.
I had a mother who read me things
That wholesome life to the boy heart brings—
Stories that stir with an upward touch.
Oh that each mother of boys were such!
You may have tangible wealth untold,
Caskets of jewels and coffers of gold.
Richer than I, you can never be,
I had a mother who read to me.

Enough said.

Be a Better Listener

A vital aspect of relationship building lies in our ability to communicate. This is true, not so much in our ability to talk (most of us have no problem with that), but in our ability to listen.

Listening is an art few of us have learned to do well. I used to think I was a good listener until I entered my graduate program in counseling. There I had to learn how to put myself—my ideas and my thoughts—on hold and focus on the individual speaking to me.

Some adults have a difficult time really listening to children. After all, they may say, "Children should be seen and not heard." Yet these same parents expect their children to listen to them. If we want our children to listen to us, we will need to teach them by example.

How often have you been busy with a project when your child interrupts what you're doing? You may encourage the child to talk while you work—and you may try to listen—but are you really focused on that child? Are you really paying attention?

How long has it been since someone really listened to you? In our society we get too busy. We're sometimes too involved in ourselves to listen to or take other people seriously. How do you feel when someone is preoccupied while you are trying to get an important point across? We are probably all guilty of not listening as carefully as we should. When we don't listen intently, we send a clear message: "I don't think what you're saying is important enough to warrant my full attention."

If you're wondering why your kids aren't listening to you, the answer may be that you have taught them how not to listen. Let's renew the true art of listening. When we stop what we are doing, look the child in the eye (this may mean getting down to his level), and are intent on listening, we are saying in effect, "I respect you. What you have to say is important to me."

Are you a good listener? Test yourself by listening to your child for five minutes. During that time be aware of how often you are tempted to interrupt with advice or an idea of your own. At the end of that time either repeat back or write down what the child said.

In counseling sessions a therapist may have to listen for forty minutes or more and at the end of that time evaluate and write a report on the session. Listening intently is hard work.

At this point, you may be saying, "My child chatters incessantly. If I took time to listen to everything she says, I'd never get anything else done." I can relate. Two of my granddaughters haven't yet learned what it means to be quiet for longer than five seconds. In cases where children talk constantly, we may occasionally need to practice selective listening. By getting to know your child, you'll learn instinctively when you really need to stop, look at your child, and listen with both ears.

The Opportunity to Parent

Parents, especially those who struggle with great needs of their own or those whose children have behavioral problems, may view parenting as a burden or an overwhelming responsibility. I admit there were times I certainly felt that way. Today, however, I view parenting and grandparenting as a wonderful opportunity to enjoy children and discover not only their unique gifts, talents, and personalities, but what children have to teach me about life.

When my husband and I held our newborn babes in our arms, we had no doubt that we had been entrusted with two of God's richest treasures. I am awed by the fact that God would give such precious gifts to us. Eventually I realized that children are not gifts—at least not in the sense of our having ownership of them. Rather, the gift comes in the opportunity God gives us to be providers and caregivers. Children don't belong to their parents. In fact the idea of ownership of a child can lead to abuse.

One father, who was brought up on abuse charges, swore he had a right to hurt his child, saying, "This is my kid. I can do what I see fit." For him, "fit" meant locking his two-year-old daughter in the closet for hours if she didn't eat her vegetables.

You can never own another human being, no more than God owns us. We are not slaves to a controlling god. Rather, we come to God because we choose to enter into a relationship with our Creator. We are never unwilling participants in our relationship with God. When we accept his gifts of love, mercy, and grace, he considers us his children. This is the way we are to relate to our children.

While writing the book *What Kids Need Most in a Mom*, I found a poem that beautifully illustrates the parent-child relationship.

> Your children are not your children.
> They are the sons and daughters
>   of Life's longing for itself.
> They come through you not from you,
> And though they are with you yet
>   they belong not to you.
> You may give them your love,

but not your thoughts,
For they have their own thoughts.
You may house their bodies,
but not their souls . . .

The Prophet
Khalil Gibran

The treasure of parenting is found in the adventure of watching children grow into unique and precious individuals under your watchful smile. For a short time we are given the reins. We are to nurture, guide and direct their paths, and, in a sense, create their world. We are responsible for making their environment safe and full of love.

Some day others will intrude into their lives with compelling arguments for immorality, greed, arrogance, and disobedience. Before that begins to happen, we must work quickly and wisely to fill their lives with love, joy, kindness, goodness, and gentleness. We must model for them patience, faithfulness, and self-control and help them develop resilience and self-esteem. We'll need to help them become self-caring, trusting, and independent enough to stand strong against the forces that would disrupt their lives.

Sadly, many of our young children have already been negatively influenced and as damaged children are themselves disruptive to others. In the next chapter we're going to talk about some what-ifs. What if you work to build strong relationships, give unconditional love, and listen with your whole being, and still the child in your care does not respond? What if you have a strong-willed, disruptive, disagreeable, or angry child who rejects the loving care you offer?

10

The Difficult Child

For three days in a row Jamie, age six, has ignored his mother's request that he come straight home from school. When confronted, he shrugs his shoulders and says, "I forgot."

His mother says, "Sometimes I feel like . . . No, I shouldn't say it. I mean, I really feel guilty about it but I've actually thought about giving him away." She hesitates and sighs. "I wouldn't, of course. I really do love him. It's just that he makes me crazy. I don't know. Maybe it's me. Maybe I'm just a lousy parent."

Marcus, age eighteen months, doesn't seem to know the meaning of the word *no*. His exasperated father shakes his head and says, "I must have pulled that kid away from the electrical outlet five times today. You'd think he'd learn. I've tried everything. What do I have to do to get him to mind?"

Kevin at ten consistently ignores the rules. He seems intent on doing the very things his parents ask him not to. "I feel like I'm constantly having to punish him," his dad complains. "I wish we could have some time together when I don't feel like we're at war with one another."

What do these children have in common? Some consider them strong willed; others see them as difficult. And to still others, these children are impossible. It seems as though from birth on they are out to get you. They test you to the limit and sometimes make you wonder why you ever decided to have children.

Being a speaker and counselor, I am often asked to do parenting workshops and seminars. When I mention the strong-willed child, eyebrows go up, heads nod in recognition, and I usually hear a series of groans. Nearly every family has at least one—that difficult child, the one who refuses to comply. Why are some children more difficult than others?

Personality plays a part. As Dr. James Dobson has written:

> They seem to be defiant upon exit from the womb. They come into the world smoking a cigar and yelling about the temperature in the delivery room and the incompetence of the nursing staff. . . . They expect meals to be served the instant they are ordered and they demand every moment of Mother's time. As months unfold, their expression of willfulness becomes even more apparent, the winds reaching hurricane force during toddlerhood.[1]

Strong-willed children present a number of problems for parents and caregivers. We are concerned about their behavior. We may ask ourselves questions like Why is my child like this? Is his behavior normal? What can I do with this kid? What am I doing wrong? Many parents struggle daily with feelings of inadequacy and an inability to cope.

What can I say? I've been there. As a parent of two strong-willed kids, I have asked all these questions and more.

Is My Child Normal?

Your strong-willed child is probably normal and is most likely going through the normal phases of growth and development and simply has a strong propensity to do things his or her own way. I remember feeling exasperated when my son was two. Until that time I thought I was a pretty effective parent. I talked to my mother-in-law about how independent and stubborn my son had become. She just smiled and said, "It gets worse." She was right.

I'm convinced that nearly all children come equipped with strong wills. Some learn early on how to lull their parents into a false sense of security. My daughter is a case in point.

Caryl came into this world crying and she didn't stop for about two months. After that, however, she was nearly perfect. At two, she potty trained herself. She was a charmer. Years later I realized Caryl had an even stronger will than her brother had. She was what many term passive resistant. In other words, she'd agree to anything you asked of her and be so convincing you wouldn't realize for hours, sometimes days, later that she hadn't done it.

It is normal for children to go through phases of crying, whining, manipulating, temper tantrums, resisting authority, refusing to be potty trained, refusing to eat, pushing the boundaries, and a hundred or so other acts we could mention. Be aware, however, that some behavior problems may suggest something more serious. An illness, disability, or other disorder can negatively affect your child's behavior.

For example, Casey, three, has hypoglycemia. At times, especially before breakfast, his blood sugar drops to dangerously low levels. His blood sugar levels greatly affect Casey's mood. When he was too young to tell his parents what was wrong, he would often whine or cry until someone fed him. At other times he'd become hostile, breaking toys and hitting at anyone within reach. Before his parents learned of his medical problem, they focused on correcting his behavior rather than on dealing with the cause. For the most part, all Casey needed to modify his behavior and mood swings was a diet that would keep his blood sugar level consistent and within the normal range.

Attachment Disorder

My friend Marcia recently wrote of her experiences with her difficult-to-manage child. "My son refused to do his homework," she began. "After a brief argument, he grabbed me around the throat. I froze in horror. When he let go, I walked over to the phone and called a man from church. 'Would you please come get John?' I asked him. 'He just tried to strangle me.'"

Thirteen years before, Marcia and her husband adopted John. "I looked at John and knew instantly he'd be ours." He'd been abandoned and abused, physically, emotionally, and sexually. Once John mentioned that his stepfather, a policeman, had hand-cuffed him to the bed when he'd done something wrong.

John was withdrawn, but the social worker assured the adop-tive parents, "All he needs is love and he'll come out of his shell and be a real part of the family."

But love and being part of a family didn't work for John. His be-havior was often bizarre. He would defecate in his closet, smear feces on the walls at school, exhibit unacceptable sexual behavior, set fires, ignore rules, and threaten his sister with a butcher knife.

As a teenager John had no interest in learning to drive, dating, working, or anything other than drawing, TV, and video games. He was an excellent artist, but would draw only violent scenes.

Marcia experienced tremendous guilt and confusion. What was wrong with this child she'd vowed to love and care for? Eventu-ally she discovered that John, like many neglected and abandoned children, had attachment disorder.

Attachment disorder is a condition in which individuals have difficulty forming loving, lasting, intimate relationships. These disorders vary in severity, but the individual shows a nearly com-plete lack of ability to be genuinely affectionate with others. He or she typically fails to develop a conscience and does not learn how to trust. As one mother in a television interview said, "These children are the future Ted Bundys of the world."

The symptoms of attachment disorder include:

- ability to be superficially engaging and charming but unable to form loving relationships.
- avoidance of eye contact
- indiscriminate affection with strangers
- inability to give and receive affection (not cuddly)

- being destructive to self and others
- cruelty to animals
- chronic lying (about the obvious)
- impulsiveness—lacking control
- learning lags and disorders
- lack of cause and effect thinking
- no conscience
- abnormal eating patterns
- poor peer relationships
- preoccupation with fire, blood, gore
- persistent nonsensical questions and incessant chatter
- being inappropriately demanding and clingy
- abnormal speech patterns

Causes of attachment disorder vary. Any of the following conditions, especially occurring to a child under eighteen months of age, put a child at high risk for developing an attachment disorder.

- maternal deprivation
- abuse (physical, emotional, sexual), neglect, and abandonment
- sudden separation from primary caretaker (such as illness or death of mother or sudden illness or hospitalization of child)
- undiagnosed and/or painful illness, such as colic or ear infections
- frequent moves and/or placements (foster care, failed adoptions)
- inconsistent or inadequate day care
- chronic maternal depression
- teenage mother with poor mothering skills

Reaching children with attachment disorder is possible but difficult. Parents and caregivers who suspect their child is exhibiting symptoms of the disorder should seek professional help. Counseling often consists of using methods that allow children to redo, in a sense, the first year or two of life. They are placed in a safe and loving environment where they can regress to infancy and hopefully develop trust and successfully bond with a parental figure.

Attention Deficit Disorder

Allergies, food additives, and certain toxins have been linked to learning disabilities and behavior problems in children. Behavior problems can also occur as a result of conditions such as attention deficit disorder (ADD).

"I feel like I'm living with a whirlwind," several mothers have said in describing life with an ADD child. An estimated 5 percent of American children have ADD. What is it? An article in *Christian Parenting Today* by Elizabeth DeBeasi gives this definition: "Attention deficit disorder is a neurobiological disability characterized by attention skills that are inappropriate, impulsive behavior, and in some cases, hyperactivity."[2]

The syndrome is called attention deficit disorder because the central problem is *inattention*, followed by *impulsivity* and *hyperactivity*. According to Dr. Paul W. Clement, professor of psychology at Fuller Theological Seminary, the symptoms include the following.[3]

Inattention
- inability to complete tasks after they are started
- behavior that suggests the child is not listening or paying attention
- being easily distracted
- difficulty sticking with assigned tasks such as schoolwork
- not sticking with a single constructive play activity

Impulsivity
- frequently acting out (at times in ways that are dangerous) without considering the consequences

- changing activities at an excessive rate
- inability to organize work at an age-appropriate level
- behaving in a way that causes adults to provide excessive supervision
- excessive speaking or yelling out in the classroom
- refusing to take turns or to wait for one's turn in games or other group activities

Hyperactivity (ADD may occur without hyperactivity.)
- constantly in motion, running, climbing—like having a mainspring that never unwinds
- fidgeting excessively, unable to sit still
- tossing and turning excessively during sleep

While the exact causes of ADD are unknown, experts assure us that it is not "something that just develops, or that is caused by emotional or physical disturbances . . . or by chaotic home environment."[4]

At this point you may be saying, "That sounds just like my kid." If so, talk to your child's doctor about your concerns and arrange to have your child tested. Author Elizabeth DeBeasi writes: "In order to make a proper diagnosis, a comprehensive evaluation should be performed by a psychiatrist and/or neurologist with input from pediatricians, teachers and parents."[5]

Be aware, however, that, as Dr. Clement warns, "stressful environments can also produce many of the behaviors which define attention deficit disorder. . . ." Dr. Clement has a good point regarding the effect of a stressful environment, a point made even stronger when we consider what the average child encounters nearly every day.

A Chaotic World

We know how important boundaries and consistency are for the proper growth and development of children. Yet many children in our country must deal not only with inconsistencies, but in some cases, complete chaos.

In the book *Whose Child?* William Kessen contends that during a visit to China he saw no "learning disabled" children and no "hyperactives." "We saw little or no squirming or thumb sucking or tics or inattention."[6]

Kessen links this finding to the philosophy of the Chinese people, which is characterized by "stability of expectations" and "a shared sense of what a child is."[7] There is a consistency of cultural values, a congruity as to how children should be reared, and a stability of the family and cultural structure. There is a general consensus about how things are done and how a child is to behave. In our society we have no such consistency.

Certainly we don't want to emulate a repressive society like that of China or force every child into the same mold, but as Kessen asks of parents and teachers: ". . . what is our fact, what is our ideology, and . . . what burden do we lay on our children to live out the tension between the two? How much does our exquisite variety cost?"[8]

Kessen says:

Children, like the rest of us, are defined by the people they meet. The social definition of children in the late twentieth-century America is a curious conglomeration: A five-year-old . . . child is one kind of person for his parents, another for his kindergarten teacher, yet another for his eurhythmics teacher, his swimming teacher, his friends, the parents of his friends, the folks in the supermarket, and his . . . grandparents. The contemporary American child is a crazy quilt of expectations and, it follows as it should, a crazy quilt of definitions. Not surprisingly, the child here and now sees himself as a polymorph, a man for any season, a magic slate on whom anybody can write a recipe.[9]

Though diversity may be the spice of life, too much may have a detrimental effect on young minds. We see this diversity in many areas. For example, what some schools teach may be entirely different from what the parents teach. Educators and parents may say they want what's best for the children, but when a child is pressed on several sides by authority figures with different values, opinions, and priorities, she may easily become confused and spilt in her loyalties. A child desperately needs to be able to trust the adults in her life, but she finds she can't trust what anyone says because everyone is saying something different. She must decide for herself, make her own rules, and find her own path. She has nothing solid to lean against or to believe in and thus becomes fearful, anxious, and insecure. She is damaged, her moral fabric frayed and hanging by a thread.

While we don't want to be alarmists or feel we have to diagnose or label every behavior, we do need to know if serious problems exist. If a child in your care seems especially difficult to manage or if you suspect an underlying medical problem, talk with a pediatrician and/or child developmental specialist.

These professionals can help you determine whether or not the child in your care is exhibiting normal behavior or if you're dealing with something more serious. It may be something that may be helped by medication or even a change in diet. In many cases children get better simply by learning how to manage their emotions and reduce stress levels.

Abuse and Difficult Children

Dealing with difficult children can stretch a parent to the limit. For some parents the stretch is too long and they break, sometimes abusing the child. In an earlier chapter I mentioned that difficult children are at high risk for abuse. This is especially true when the child's parents are also high risk; that is, if they were victims of abuse or are egocentric, severely stressed, low-income, needy, isolated, and/or have no support system (see information about high-risk parents in chapter 4).

In my research I came across some interesting statistics on this topic of abuse as it pertains to the difficult child. Svea J. Gold, author of *When Children Invite Child Abuse,* says:

There are many abused and beaten children who have grown up and, to all outward appearances, are normal human beings. We know very little about them. The one group which has been studied from all angles and on whom we have all kinds of statistics is the prison population.[10]

According to the Child Abuse Council, of the prisoners studied:

1. All were abused as children.
2. A majority, about 75 percent, were learning disabled.
3. Eighty percent had hypoglycemia (symptoms of hypoglycemia include mood swings, anxiety attacks, and incoherent thoughts).

The findings, though certainly inconclusive, suggest a relationship between difficult-to-manage children and abuse. They also bring up some interesting questions about the relationship between illness and learning disabilities. Undoubtedly in many cases, genetics and personality play a major role in how a child turns out. But how many disturbed and problematic children in our society today have become so as a result of poor parenting skills, abuse, and neglect? As Gold says, "any child, given the wrong nutrition or a barren, nonstimulating environment, can be turned into a learning-disabled or otherwise deficient child."[11]

Eight-year-old Ben exemplifies what Gold is saying.

"I don't know if I can take much more," Crystal said. "I'm not sure I have what it takes to care for a troubled kid."

She and her husband had opened their home to Ben, who had lived in an abusive home for five years where he was threatened, lied to, and beaten by an alcoholic stepfather. "He's so disruptive and sometimes I'm afraid he's going to hurt the other children. Sometimes I'm afraid *I'm* going to hurt him. I know life has been hard for him, but why isn't he responding to our love? He just doesn't seem to be getting any better. I'm beginning to wonder if there's any hope. At least now I can empathize with his parents," Crystal finished. "He's impossible."

Ben, like many children who have been abused, acts out his confusion, distrust, and anger in an almost frenzied behavior. He

111

is intense and anxious and he seems bound for destruction. According to his biological mother, Ben has always been a difficult child to handle. He was born prematurely and had numerous physical problems during his first three years.

During that time, his parents fought a great deal, mostly over money problems, and ended up divorced. Ben's father eventually faded from the picture. His mother remarried and Ben's stepfather constantly criticized, threatened, and severely punished him. His mother finally asked for help from a counseling agency. Eventually Ben was placed in foster care.

Ben now carries the tag "difficult child" with him. Though he is now physically healthy and is being well treated by his foster parents, Ben continues to act out his role as a "bad boy."

Crystal says, "He's so defiant and downright mean at times. It's almost like he's asking for trouble."

Undoubtedly some of Ben's behavioral problems can be traced to past abuse. But there is also evidence to suggest Ben's early illness and perhaps even his personality were contributing factors in the abuse. I'm not suggesting he was in any way responsible for it. Children, though they may deliberately defy their parents, are never to blame for the abuse they may incur as a result of an adult's response to them. No matter how a child acts, the full responsibility for abuse lies with the adult.

However, there is a possibility that Ben, being a difficult-to-manage child, became a catalyst for the abuse. In other words, had he been healthy, happy, and compliant, he may have escaped abuse.

Getting Help

Anna loved her children, but at times she found them, especially two-year-old Danny, more then she could handle. One evening she came home from work exhausted. While she was trying to prepare dinner, Danny grabbed her legs and wouldn't let go. "Mommy, hold me."

"I don't have time right now, Danny. Go play in the other room."

"No! I want you now."

She pushed him away and he came back to her, wanting to be picked up. "Something snapped," Anna sobbed as she related her story. "I just kept hitting him again and again."

Finally Danny curled up on the floor, sobbing, "Don't hurt me no more. I be good."

Horrified and ashamed at what she had done, Anna gathered Danny in her arms and tearfully tried to comfort him.

The combination of stress, the inability to cope, and a child who can't or won't cooperate can send even the most empathic and devoted parent over the edge. But mix a high-risk child and a high-risk parent together and you have the elements of an abusive cycle. Parents with difficult-to-manage children need the support of a trusted family member or friend to call when they're feeling overwhelmed.

In chapter 16, I offer advice on helping parents through parenting classes and support groups. This support isn't only for the high-risk, or abusive, parents. It's for all of us—parents, grandparents, foster and adoptive parents, teachers—anyone who cares for difficult-to-manage children.

It may be hard for some of us to admit we need help, especially if we're experienced in child rearing and in a position of leadership in the community. After all, we're the ones with the expertise. We should be able to handle any child. Right?

I see myself as a pretty decent parent and grandparent. After all, I worked as a pediatric nurse for more than fifteen years, reared two strong-willed kids with varying degrees of success, and hold a master of arts degree in counseling. Yet until recently, my five-year-old granddaughter, Kyrstin, had me baffled. She's adorable and has the face of an angel but that child is one of the most willful, defiant, and persistent children I have ever met. And I mean that in the nicest way.

The other day, after listening to her high-pitched voice for nearly an hour—the one she uses to make her dolls talk—I asked her to play quietly for a while. She readily agreed. Her idea of quiet, however, was to lower her voice about one decibel and to keep talking. She jabbered on as though her mouth was stuck in the "on" position and it seemed that nothing short of a battery failure would turn her off.

Kyrstin has a dynamite smile that she uses to charm you every time you tell her not to do something, like running in the house. She hesitates, flashes you a smile, turns her engine down a notch, and keeps right on going.

She's the kind of child that I imagine even Jesus would find exasperating. Well, probably not, but I sure do. Dealing with Kyrstin reminds me of an important fact. I don't have all the answers.

Caring for children should not be a solo operation but a cooperative effort. If you feel yourself coming close to the edge, don't be afraid to reach out and ask for help. And if you're on the helping side, avoid criticism, placing blame, and/or offering unwanted advice. Instead, empathize, listen, and if you have some ideas that might help, share them in a respectful, loving way.

We've talked about various aspects of the difficult child in this chapter and learned that these children run a higher risk of being abused than the more easy-care kids. The abuse can occur not only from parents, but foster parents, teachers, and others who become overwhelmed, don't understand, or don't have proper training. In closing this chapter, I'd like to share a story of a boy who is labeled "behavior disordered."

Cody's mother, Dana, was young and inexperienced. She did her best to care for him, but as he grew older and got into more trouble, she found it harder to cope with him. She sought counseling and worked hard to be the mother Cody needed. Her difficulties involved not only an active little boy, but also an alcoholic husband.

Dana isn't certain how it happened; maybe it was not having a dad around, or having a dad who didn't care, but Cody grew into an angry and confused little boy. In school his teachers had trouble handling him and in the second grade labeled him "learning disabled." They placed him in a special education unit and bused him to a school twenty miles away from his home. One day Cody misbehaved on the hour-and-a-half ride home. The bus driver, determined to show the kid who was boss, forced Cody into a straightjacket. The incident so terrified the child that his behavior problems multiplied as a result.

Two years later, during an especially difficult time, Dana followed the suggestion of a counselor and placed Cody in a foster home for a short time. When Dana went to visit, she found him dirty and unkempt. The foster mother had abused him. It took Dana several days to get her son back. The system designed to help children like Cody had failed him again.

Recently, a bus driver hit Cody for being disruptive and barred him from riding her bus. Shortly after that he was kicked out of school. His teacher gave no reason other than that he was afraid Cody would become angry and injure one of the other children and the parents would sue the school. Cody had liked his teacher and as a result felt rejected. But that was nothing new. People had been rejecting him since he was born.

Dana, after months of fighting the school system, sought legal help and threatened to file suit against the school unless something was done to assure her son a proper education.

Cody, now twelve, attends a special school and is transported daily by a caring woman who says Cody behaves wonderfully. Cody is a bright and sensitive boy, but to some he has been a problem child. Cody has suffered a great deal of abuse by people who didn't know how to cope with and care for a difficult child.

Parents and caregivers of difficult-to-manage children will want to carefully monitor all the people, such as teachers and counselors, who care for their children. These children can be hard to deal with but not impossible, and it's important to find people who can care for them with skill and love.

The community has a responsibility to the difficult-to-manage child and his or her parents and must have the resources available for consistent support and understanding.

11

PLANS FOR PARENTING
THE DIFFICULT CHILD

"We have two kids, Megan, three, and Joshua, six," a frustrated young mother shared. "Megan is every parent's dream child. She's easygoing and hardly ever cries, but Joshua is always on the move. He can't sit still for two seconds and gets into everything. Don't get me wrong. I love Josh but at times I feel like locking him in a cage. He drives me to distraction. We have tried every kind of discipline. Nothing seems to work. I feel like a total failure as a parent."

We have seen the special needs of the difficult child. In this chapter and the next I'll talk about ways to provide care for these children and assist them in caring for themselves. Helping the difficult child involves two approaches: (1.) helping parents and caregivers to cope, and (2.) providing care and guidance for the child. One of the first problems we need to deal with in caring for difficult children is the guilt feelings that parents often have.

What Am I Doing Wrong?

Parents often blame themselves for behavioral problems in their children. For many conscientious parents, feelings of guilt can become so strong they inhibit their efforts to parent well. These parents may become so overwhelmed by fear of inadequacy that they fail to trust their instincts and intuition.

If you care about your kids and if you love them unconditionally and are doing your best to meet their needs and provide a safe, nurturing environment, you probably have no reason to feel guilty. As Dr. Dobson says, "the willful child can be difficult to control even when his parents handle him with great skill and dedication. It takes several years to bring him to a point of relative obedience and cooperation within the family unit."[1] Even though Dr. Dobson isn't speaking specifically of abused children or children with learning disabilities, the basic principle applies. He also tells parents not to panic or try to transform the child overnight.

One of the greatest sources of guilt may come from people outside the family who don't understand. Bill O'Conner, father of two hyperactive children, says:

> What they see is a child who is often out of control. They'll blame the child, and they'll blame you. Explain where you can, apologize when necessary, discipline your child when appropriate. But don't allow your child to be too harshly criticized. And try not to carry the weight of outside judgment on your shoulders.[2]

In addition, many parents set themselves up for guilt by expecting too much from themselves and their children. Sometimes parents need to loosen their standards, particularly if they lean toward perfectionism. Basically we need to remember that we're probably not going to eliminate all of the problems our children have. Consider yourself fortunate if you and your child can find acceptable ways to minimize the most harmful and disruptive ones.

Avoid unjustly criticizing yourself for making mistakes. Just as a potter doesn't sit down at the wheel and expertly throw a perfect bowl or plate on the first try, neither should a parent expect to be an expert immediately. It takes about seven years to become a master potter and that involves a great deal of practice and study of all types of clays and glazes.

With children the work is much the same. There is no magic button to push in our brains or our hearts that shifts us into a parenting mode. And as any parent will tell you, rearing one child does not necessarily equip you to handle the next one with more expertise. A potter who works with stoneware for several years, then switches to porcelain can't expect the same techniques to produce the same results. He needs to learn many new techniques because the clay has different qualities.

As a wise parent once stated, "Before I was married I had six theories about bringing up children. Now I have six children and no theories" (Lord Rochester, 1647–1680).

All children, regardless of whether they have been abused, will exhibit some behavior problems. We do ourselves and our children a disfavor by expecting otherwise. We need to set realistic expectations. We will undoubtedly make mistakes—so will our children. Be willing to acknowledge your wrongs and ask for forgiveness. Set the guilt aside and get on with your life. Give yourself permission to be a less-than-perfect parent.

Be Objective

One of the ways in which parents can better cope with their children is by being objective and by giving an empathic response.[3] As I mentioned in chapter 5, this means responding to your child by focusing on his or her needs and how you can meet those needs, rather than on yourself and what the child's behavior is doing to you.

To accomplish objectivity, you may need to get away from the child and your emotions for a brief time. Take time out to think about what's happening so you can respond rationally. When we respond as emotionally healthy adults, we are able to empathize with or "feel" that child's need—to understand, identify, and meet that need.

Our goal is to maintain enough emotional distance from the need to be able to satisfy it. When your child misbehaves don't think of yourself as a failure or worry about how you will look to others. Focus on the child. Say to yourself, *My child has a need*

*right now. I want to determine what that need is and then decide
how best to meet it.*

Have Confidence in Yourself

It can be easy to lose confidence in yourself when you're dealing with a difficult child. I went into parenting armed with all the
latest child care manuals. I knew all about effective discipline and
positive reinforcement. I was determined to be a good parent and
as a result my child would be well behaved. Unfortunately my children hadn't read the same books.

Parenting never has been or ever will be as easy as finding the
right techniques. As child psychiatrist, Stanley Turecki, director
of the Difficult Child Center in New York City, says, "There's no
one ideal technique that suits every temperament."

Whatever techniques you use, act confident. Don't let your kids
see you sweat. You may feel unsure of yourself but you don't want
your child to even suspect you may be wavering. The moment you
do, he'll think he's found a vulnerable spot and go in for the kill. As
Dobson tells us, "Nothing is more destructive to parental leadership
than for a mother or father to disintegrate during that struggle."[4]

Children need to see you strong and confident in order to feel safe
and secure. They may fight you every inch of the way, but if your child
wins the battle, you may both lose the war.

This doesn't mean you are to do battle with your child over
every broken rule or misbehavior. You'll need to determine in advance which rules are negotiable and which are not. For example, one nonnegotiable rule would be, We don't play in the street.
Another might be, We don't hit the baby.

Build your self-esteem as a parent by being open and honest
with other adults about your difficulties. The Bible tells us to encourage one another and bear one another's burdens. As you do
that, you'll find many kindred spirits. Share battle stories as well
as techniques you've found that work.

Husbands and wives will want to work toward a strong marital relationship in which they can resolve conflicts that arise in

parenting difficult-to-manage children. And there will be conflicts. Work at presenting a united front. Be consistent whenever possible. If possible, spend time together away from the kids once a week to concentrate on loving, supporting, and encouraging each other.

Avoid criticizing yourself, your mate, or your kids. You'll need to be careful not to give your children the wrong impression of yourselves or them. As my daughter once asked, "If you guys think you've failed as parents, then does that mean you think I'm a failure as a kid?" Ouch!

While you try to be positive about yourselves and your parenting skills, save some good thoughts for that difficult child.

Maintaining a Positive Attitude

Many of us tend to think in negative terms about children who present a challenge, and our parenting style often reflects that negative attitude. Think about the terms we sometimes use to describe these difficult-to-manage children. These are the kids who "have a mind of their own" or who "give their parents a bad time." We talk about the "terrible twos" and "rebellious teens." We might use the terms *stubborn, belligerent, ornery, argumentative,* or *disruptive.* I'm sure you can think of a word or two of your own.

Instead of using critical words to describe a child's behavior or, in some cases, his nature, we may do well to use more positive words like *determined, persistent, imaginative, curious, motivated, dynamic, persuasive,* and *assertive.* This may put us in the frame of mind where we can help a child channel an unacceptable behavior into a more appropriate behavior.

Respect a child's uniqueness and self-reliance. Admire her strengths. Determination, persistence, resilience, and motivation are the things leaders are made of. Many children whom parents see as difficult often display leadership qualities. Teach your child to use her skills in socially acceptable ways. Here are some suggestions.

- Put your defiant child in charge of a project you know he can handle.

- Suggest that your four year old lead the way on a family hike.
- Ask your six year old to direct a puppet play.
- Encourage an older child to run for an office or lead a youth group.
- Be creative. Know your child's gifts and talents and provide ways for him or her to shine.

Children need positive feedback. We will need to catch our difficult kids doing good things and give them lots of positive reinforcement and praise. Avoid taking the child's good behavior for granted. Notice when he is well behaved as well as when he is not. Some experts I've read suggest that children need at least three praises and positive remarks for each criticism.

The Will to Survive

While we're looking at positives, I'd like to focus for a moment on the strong-willed child. The strong-willed child has gotten a lot of bad press. Exasperated parents wring their hands and set out to change that strong will into compliance. True, a compliant child may be easier to live with, but before you take it upon yourself to tame your child's will, there's something I'd like you to think about. A strong will is not necessarily a bad thing. In fact it may be a child's most valuable asset.

It's true that the willful or defiant child can be a handful, but let's look on the bright side. A strong will has its benefits, and if we are wise, we will learn to help children use their strength of will to overcome adversity. The will helps us accomplish the developmental task of autonomy—gaining independence or separateness from one's parents. I also see it as a basic tool for survival and a strong determinant for resilience—the ability to bounce back. A strong will can help a child overcome obstacles and persevere in the face of severe trauma.

I think of three-year-old Jesse, who fell into a raging river while on a white-water rafting trip. His father and uncle died in the rafting accident, but Jesse tenaciously clung to a rock for two hours until someone rescued him.

In a similar incident, a six-year-old girl jumped into a river to try to save her drowning father. She couldn't help him but swam to a buoy and held on until help came several hours later. Rescuers said they couldn't believe she had survived.

In another astonishing story, a mother died in a car accident. Three-year-old Amanda survived fourteen hours in zero-degree temperatures, barefoot and in a lightweight coat, by cuddling up to her mother's body. When rescuers found her, she cried, "My mommy's dead!"

For these children to survive their ordeals, it took a powerful inner force and a strong will to live. This is the same tenacity that can help damaged children overcome the difficulties life throws in their paths.

A strong will can help children survive. But let's look at the will in general. As people created in God's image, we each come equipped with a will and it is a good thing. As Bernard of Clairvaux (a twelfth-century theologian) wisely stated: "I discover three distinct faculties of my soul that enable me to remember, contemplate, and desire God. These are the faculties of memory, understanding, and *will*. By the first of these faculties, I recollect. By the second I discern. By the third, [the will] I love and embrace God" (italics mine).

The will is an inherent quality or drive, designed by God, that is meant to parallel and be conformed to God's will. The stronger that will, the stronger our adherence to God can be. Unfortunately, we all too frequently make unhealthy choices that deter the will and bend it in the wrong direction—away from God.

It seems, then, our job as parents is not to weaken or break the will, but to nurture, encourage, correct, and guide our child's will toward God. We will also want to help children channel their energy into ways that will help them resolve their problems.

Parenting is a serious responsibility and one that takes a tremendous amount of time and effort. Yet it is one of the most important jobs we'll ever have. As child care specialist Marlene Canter says, "Children are the hope for the future, but we are the hope for theirs."

12

EFFECTIVE DISCIPLINE

"One of the things I struggle with," says Marcia, a foster parent, "is how to discipline a child who has been abused."

Marcia's concerns are very real. After all, we wouldn't want to inadvertently do something that might harm even more the child in our care. For the most part, we can discipline broken children in much the same way we discipline any child—carefully. If a child has been severely abused, you may need to work with a counselor or child development specialist to formulate a care plan that includes effective discipline methods.

Discipline can be a scary thing for many parents, and it's easy to see why. Nearly everyone you talk to has a different opinion. I have an opinion as well. While I don't claim to have all the answers, I have, over the years, developed some commonsense rules you may find helpful.

I have four rules for parents concerning discipline.

1. Adopt methods you feel are best for you and your child.
2. Realize that what works for one child won't necessarily work for the next.
3. Work for conformity and consistency of discipline methods among all those who care for the child.
4. Always discipline with an attitude of love, remembering the words of the apostle Paul:

Love is patient, love is kind. It does not envy, it does not boast, it is not proud. It is not rude, it is not self-seeking, it is not easily angered, it keeps no record of wrongs. Love does not delight in evil but rejoices with the truth. It always protects, always trusts, always hopes, always perseveres.

1 Corinthians 13:4–7

Defining Discipline

One of the problems many parents have in the area of discipline is that they see discipline as a necessary evil, something they'd rather not deal with. Consequently children today are often undisciplined and running scared. Just the other day a friend of mine told me about a six-year-old child who kept hitting her while she and the child's mother were talking. The mother totally ignored the child's actions. "He was an obnoxious brat," my friend said. "I felt like I should have done something, but it wasn't really the kid's fault. His mom obviously doesn't know a thing about discipline."

Every child needs a parent who loves him enough to discipline him wisely. How do we do that? Perhaps one of the first keys to effective discipline is understanding what it actually means. Many tend to use the words *discipline* and *punishment* synonymously. Although discipline may include chastisement, correction, punishment, and penalty, it has far deeper implications. To discipline also means to guide, instruct, train, prepare, indoctrinate, develop, moderate, and restrain. It implies a state of orderliness, habit, regimen, and adherence to certain rules, as opposed to the chaos, confusion, and disorderliness of the undisciplined.

Effective discipline then must incorporate not only forms of punishment, but also methods for teaching and guiding a child into an orderly and self-disciplined way of life. Discipline is something we do *for* our children, not something we do *to* them. I was reading a devotional the other day, and came across these words by Hannah Whitall Smith: "If love sees those it loves going wrong,

124

it must, because it is love, do what it can to save them. Any supposed love that would fail to do this is really selfishness."

When parents guide, instruct, and correct their children in love, they are giving their children a place in which to develop the trust and security they so desperately need.

Something else that may help put the idea of loving discipline into perspective is a little advice from the experts. A team of fifteen researchers, headed by Dr. Burton L. White, conducted, from 1965 to 1975, an intensive study of toddlers (ages eight to eighteen months), known as the Harvard University Preschool Project. Their goal was to learn which early childhood experiences contributed to the development of healthy, intelligent human beings.[1]

The conclusions of the study were first reported in the *APA Monitor.*[2]

1. It is increasingly clear that the origins of human competence are to be found in a critical period of development between eight and eighteen months of age. The child's experiences during these brief months do more to influence future intellectual competence than any time before or after.

2. The single most important environmental factor in the life of the child is his mother (or primary caregiver).[3] "She [or he] is on the hook," said Dr. White, and carries more influence on her (his) child's experiences than any other person or circumstance.

3. The amount of live language directed to a child (not to be confused with television, radio, or overheard conversation) is vital to his development of fundamental linguistic, intellectual, and social skills. The researchers concluded, "Providing a rich social life for a twelve- to fifteen-month-old child is the best thing you can do to guarantee a good mind."

4. Those children who are given free access to living areas of their homes progress much faster than those whose movements are restricted.

5. The nuclear family is the most important educational delivery system. If we are going to produce capable, healthy

children, it will be by strengthening family units and by improving the interactions that occur within them.

6. The best parents were those who excelled at three key functions:

- They were superb designers and organizers of their child's environment.
- They permitted their children to interrupt them for brief thirty-second episodes, during which personal consultation, comfort, information, and enthusiasm were exchanged.
- "They were firm disciplinarians while simultaneously showing great affection for their children."

As you can see, love and discipline go hand in hand and are necessary to the developing child. No matter what a child's age, effective discipline combined with love is essential to her physical, emotional, and spiritual well-being.

Setting Boundaries

One of the most important parts of discipline is the setting of boundaries. All children need boundaries designed to provide safety and an opportunity for growth. They also need to learn how to stay within those boundaries. Gregory Bodenhamer says in his book *Back in Control,* "Children aren't born wanting to obey—or disobey—the rules set down by parents, schools, or society. And one of the greatest stumbling blocks in getting children to behave *properly* is the human desire to do as one pleases." He goes on to give what he calls Bodenhamer's Law: "Human beings (including children) prefer doing things in their own way, in their own time, and given an option, will sometimes do as they please."[4]

We discipline wisely by establishing and enforcing fair and realistic boundaries. Janet Pais writes: "If children encounter nothing firm in their human environment, they will be confused, anxious, lacking boundaries, lacking a sense of reality. They will not be able to develop as solid, real, sane human beings."[5]

Children need to feel safe and secure yet have ample space to grow and develop, to experiment and explore the world in which they live. Boundaries tell a child what is acceptable and what is not. Few children today have firm boundaries. As I mentioned in chapter 10, their lives are full of inconsistencies. It is always in the best interest of a child to provide, as much as possible, a structured environment and constant routine. You'll find some suggestions to help you achieve this later in the chapter.

There is more to setting boundaries, however, than drawing a line and saying you can't cross it. Setting limits entails much more than telling your child no. While we teach children to respect the boundaries we establish, we must also teach them to develop and respect their own.

Personal Boundaries

Boundaries also serve to establish limits as to what we can or cannot do with respect to relating to or touching one another. They are, in a sense, parameters, which protect our human dignity and our human rights. Everyone has boundaries that others should respect. Healthy adults set up boundaries that keep them from harming others. They also establish boundaries to keep others from violating them.

Children need their own physical space—a room and/or space where others do not intrude. This applies to certain parts of their bodies as well. When threatened or hurt, children need to know they have the right to say, "No, you can't touch me there. You can't do that to me. I'm telling."

We can accomplish this business of establishing boundaries for ourselves and one another by simply invoking two timeless principles:

1. Love one another as Christ has loved you.
2. Treat others as you want others to treat you.

We bring the principles home by always asking ourselves and our children, "Would God want me to do this?" and "Would I want someone to do this to me?" One of the most important aspects of any relationship is knowing where to draw the line.

To Spank or Not to Spank

Ultimately when the discussion of discipline or setting boundaries comes up, so does the issue of spanking. Everyone has an opinion. Is it appropriate? Is it effective? While spanking may or may not work for some children, my personal view is that spanking a child should be a last-resort measure and preferably should not be used at all.

My concern is not for the loving parents who sometimes spank when their child deliberately or willfully disobeys. My concern is for parents who go too far—who spank too hard or too often. My concern is for children who are injured physically and emotionally by the act.

Not long ago I read of a woman who spanked her six-month-old baby with a switch because she thought it was the godly thing to do. She'd been told "Spare the rod and spoil the child" but she didn't know that a six-month-old baby was far too young to understand the rules.

I think we need to be careful in advocating a potentially harmful act. Surprisingly some of the strongest advocates for spanking are Christians. The argument for it is often Proverbs 22:15: "Folly [foolishness] is bound up in the heart of a child, but the rod of discipline will drive it far from him"; or Proverbs 29:15: "The rod of correction imparts wisdom, but a child left to himself disgraces his mother."

Proverbs is full of wise sayings, and I certainly don't discount the value in them, but to make a case for spanking based on verses out of the Old Testament may not necessarily work in our society today. If we are to follow Old Testament teachings to the letter, shouldn't we do more than choose certain verses to back up our traditions and beliefs? For example, Proverbs was written out of human wisdom and godly inspiration, but in Leviticus 18–21 we find the letter of the law and specific punishments given to Moses by God. One that particularly strikes me is "If anyone curses his father or mother, he must be put to death" (Lev. 20:9). According to the Old Testament, many sins we and our children commit are punishable by death, but we certainly are not going to insert those verses into our parenting manuals.

When Christ came, he gave us a new way to deal with such problems. Christ took our sins on himself and suffered death in our place. We now have the way of confession and forgiveness. When faced with the decision of whether or not to use spanking as a means of getting children to mind, I prefer to seek guidance from the teachings of Christ. To be honest, I have a very difficult time imagining Jesus as one who would resort to hitting a child as a means of discipline.

I have another concern. Spanking in some states is considered child abuse. I've heard of a number of cases where a parent has spanked a child and been turned in to authorities for child abuse. It may not be fair but it happens.

Finally, being spanked may teach children to use hitting as a means of dealing with problems. "If Mom hits me when I do something wrong, I can hit my brother or my friend when he's doing something wrong." Of course we don't allow our children to hit others, so we need to ask ourselves if we are setting a double standard. All too often, spanking is an act of aggression or hostility. We need to ask ourselves if this is what we want to instill in our children.

I've pointed out some concerns I have, but the rest is up to you. Spanking is an issue you'll want to devote some thought to. Read differing viewpoints. If you were spanked as a child, think about how it affected you. Did it accomplish the intended purpose? Pray for guidance. Ask God to give you a Christ-like heart as you deal with your children. Then set guidelines for the discipline of your children. These guidelines might include the following.

- Never spank a child who is under two years old or over six years old.
- Never use an object—strap, switch, or paddle—for spanking, only your hand.
- If you spank, hit only the padded flesh on the buttocks.

- Never spank when you are angry or highly stressed.
- Don't spank when you have other options for discipline.

My advice to parents regarding spanking is to avoid it. Instead, be creative. Talk with your child and come up with measures that will be effective.

As you develop effective discipline methods, you'll need to keep a firm grip and a flexible heart. Avoid rigidity. Rigor mortis is the stiffening of muscles when the body is dead. It should not happen to our hearts and brains—especially while we're alive.

All too often, in an effort to protect our children or maintain control over them, concerned parents may tighten their grip, which often has the opposite effect. Holding kids too tightly can cause resistance. Did I say resistance? Overly controlled kids, especially if they tend to be defiant, can be like mules—they plant their feet and refuse to budge.

To avoid a conflict of wills consider the following suggestions:

- Let your child know what the rules are and that you are the one in charge. Children need to know what adults expect, and until they are well versed in the rules, children need to be reminded of them on a regular basis.
- Make your rules clear and concise. Avoid long, detailed explanations.
- Strive for consensus in the disciplining methods used by Mom, Dad, babysitters, grandparents, and others. Too many differing thoughts on how to bring up a child can be confusing and chaotic for the child. The Bible tells us that a house divided against itself won't stand (see Matthew 12:25).
- Scoldings or explanations should be short and to the point (three minutes max).
- Implement logical consequences. If a child throws a temper tantrum at the toy store, go home without a toy.
- When applicable, expect restitution.
- Be firm yet flexible. Decide what's really important to you. Choose your battles.

- Be consistent. Don't keep changing the rules or the way in which you follow through.
- Don't make idle threats. As one mother aptly put it, "Say what you're going to do and do what you say."
- Don't make unreasonable demands. For example, you wouldn't spank a child for wetting the bed.

As you develop your plan for effective discipline, you'll want to decide which behaviors to allow or prohibit. Choose your limits wisely and make certain you can follow through on the limits you do set.

Be assertive and confident but not aggressive. Try not to yell. At a parenting workshop I went to, the speaker made this vivid point. "Trying to train children by yelling at them is like trying to drive your car by blowing the horn."

Parents who yell, hit, or frighten children are out of control and often lose their ability to be effective. Dr. Ross Campbell in his book *How to Really Love Your Child* says, "Anytime you start yelling and screaming or start lecturing or become negative with your child . . . you are telling him that what he has done wrong is your responsibility—not his. You are preventing him from taking responsibility."[6]

You are also giving your child a dangerous edge. You are in a sense saying, "You have the power to make me lose control." Now, tell me, what kid is going to kindly ignore that message?

Look beyond the Behavior

Kids usually misbehave for a reason. Sometimes they are testing you and the limits you've placed on them. Draw a line and they'll probably step over it. It's almost as if they are saying, "I need to know if you mean what you say. I need to know if I can trust you."

Dr. Dobson says, "When a child behaves in ways that are disrespectful or harmful to himself or others, his hidden purpose is often to verify the stability of the boundaries." At other times he may be letting you know he is tired or hungry or that he needs attention.

This is the case for Chris, age four. Chris's mother recently took a job outside the home. Getting out the door in the morning is the most frustrating and draining part of the day. Chris never wants to get up. He'd rather eat breakfast at home than eat at the day care center. He stalls and pokes around until his parents threaten to take him to day care in his underwear.

Chris doesn't want his mornings rifled with conflict. Most likely, he just wants things back the way they were with leisurely mornings and Mom at home. He may not be able to verbalize his feelings to Mom and Dad. In fact he may not even know why he's upset. So he acts out his feelings through his behavior.

Instead of asking, "Why is he being so stubborn?" Chris's parents should ask, "Why is Chris upset?" "What is he trying to say or to achieve, and how can we help him?" In other words, put yourself in your child's place and try to think like a kid (an empathetic response).

Chris is resisting the changes in his life. He's trying his best to make things like they used to be. Obviously he can't do that, but Mom and Dad can empathize with him and perhaps help him resolve his problem. Here are some things Chris's parents can try:

- Try getting Chris up a little earlier in the morning so he can be more leisurely about getting ready.
- Crawl into bed with him in the morning or have him crawl in with you so that he can begin the day being snuggled and feeling loved.
- Use the early morning quiet time to talk about feelings. The peaceful time in the evening just before sleep is also a good time for warm and positive heart-to-heart talks.
- Have most things ready to go the night before so the family can have a relaxed breakfast and talk before having to leave.

Looking beyond the behavior doesn't mean you need to stop and psychoanalyze every problem. Just try to always empathize with your child and ask, *What does my child need?*

Maybe this prayer written from a child's perspective can help.[7]

A Child's Prayer

Treat me as Mary and Joseph must have treated Jesus.

Enter into relationship with me and be guided by the divine Father-Child relationship revealed in the Gospels.

Take care of my needs.

Give me structures and limits that let me know you care.

Protect me from harm.

Love me. Hold me. Value me.

Let me know I am your beloved daughter (son), that you are well pleased with me, and that you know I am worth listening to.

Respect me and my feelings and my perceptions of reality.

Do not have contempt for me.

Do not lie to me.

Do not use me or abuse me.

Do not exercise power over me just to show me that you are the boss.

Do not try to break my will or my spirit.

Do not belittle my need for attention or my other needs.

Teach me about the world and help me to learn about myself, but do not poison me with the belief that there is something evil or contemptible about me. And do not expect perfection of yourself or of me.

Do not try to teach me how to be good, how to be God's child, or how to be me. Instead, through relationship with me, help me to know who and what I am.

Recognize that only I can let you know who I am.

Take a genuine interest in me, in how I feel and how I view things.

Be yourself and let me be me.

Trust me to grow into the human being God created me to be.

Teach me about God and how precious I am to him.

Ten Tips for Training Tots

1. *Love unconditionally.* Make 1 Corinthians 13:4–7 a foundation on which you establish your rules and guidelines.
2. *Let your child know what you expect.* As Dr. Dobson says, "If you haven't defined it—don't enforce it." Never punish a child for mistakes or accidents.
3. *Maintain order.* Children thrive on routine and consistency. Establish routines and try to follow them.
4. *Stand your ground.* When a child deliberately defies you or challenges your authority, respond with confidence. Don't argue or back down. If your son kicks you, stop him immediately. Take a firm hold of his foot and say, "Stop!" Then, after he's calm, you might ask why he is upset or explain briefly why his behavior won't be tolerated.
5. *Be fair and just.* If a child's misbehavior warrants punishment, make certain the punishment is just, fair, and humane. The punishment should match the crime.
6. *Don't argue.* When you are standing firmly on established rules, there's no need for argument or discussion. Trying to find out from a child why she has misbehaved is usually pointless. Chances are she hasn't a clue. And she probably wouldn't tell you if she did know.
7. *Be resourceful.* Don't be afraid to experiment to find a method of discipline that works best for you and your child. There are no hard-and-fast rules. Once you decide what parenting style works best for you and your child, be consistent and follow through.
8. *Express your love and reassurance.* Tell your child often that you love him. Show him your love in ways he appreciates. When there has been conflict, Dr. Dobson suggests you take time to "hold him close and tell him of your love. Let him know, again, why he was punished and how he can avoid the trouble next time. These moments can build love, fidelity, and family unity."
9. *Never punish a child for showing his emotions.* Give your child ways to express feelings and vent anger. Have her draw, paint, color, mold clay, play the piano. Physical activity—such as a hike in the woods, running, dancing, or playing catch—can also help. If she's old enough, help her verbalize her feelings.
10. *Pray.* Pray for your child and with your child. God is the divine parent who will guide and direct your path as you guide and direct your child.

Dealing with Anger

In spite of our best intentions, we become angry with our kids. Sometimes their behavior warrants our anger. It's okay to get angry with your child, says Katherine Gordy Levine, as long as you CARE:

C = Calm down
A = Ally with your child
R = Review what upset you
E = End on a positive note[8]

Anger is not necessarily a bad thing. God has shown anger. Anger can be used for good, as Christ used it in clearing out the temple and in chastising his disciples for their attitude toward children. Anger can urge us to right wrongs. But anger can also destroy.

Though rare, anger can be triggered by a physiological impairment—a chemical imbalance, a quirk in the brain, an allergy, or a medication.

Usually, anger is our response to things that have gone wrong. According to Dr. Gary Collins, people respond angrily to the following.

- *Injustice*—when we witness or hear about the rights of others being violated.
- *Frustration*—encountering obstacles we can't get around, problems we can't seem to resolve, goals and deadlines we can't meet.
- *Being threatened or hurt*—being afraid, being treated unfairly, or feeling rejected, ignored, criticized, and humiliated. Anger is often a secondary emotion following these experiences. Collins tells us that "threats like these challenge our self-esteem, remind us of our imperfections or limitations, and make us feel so vulnerable" that we end up using anger and aggression to fight back.

- *Certain circumstances*—responding in anger as we've seen others do. Anger can be a learned response. Cultures differ in their use and abuse of anger, and children imitate adults and respond in kind. Chances are, where you see an angry child, you'll encounter an angry parent. Scripture bears this out in Proverbs 22:24–25: "Do not make friends with a hot-tempered man, do not associate with one easily angered, or you may learn his ways and get yourself ensnared."[9]

Sadly our children have no choice about being with an angry parent. We often see anger acted out in children and adults who have been or are being mistreated. We tend to deal with anger in three destructive ways:

- *We avoid it.* We refuse to deal with anger or acknowledge its existence. Some try to escape it by using drugs or alcohol to hide a problem. This may work temporarily but it is like holding back a flood with cardboard. The anger builds up, eventually the dam will collapse, and the results can be devastating.
- *We turn it inward.* Sometimes we push anger down inside of ourselves and deny it even exists. But anger is like a cancer that eats away at our resolve. Anger directed at ourselves can create physical conditions such as intestinal problems, high blood pressure, headaches, and so on. It can also produce emotional problems such as depression and anxiety and can, in some cases, lead to suicide. Anger driven inward can deprive the soul of joy and produce the fruits of bitterness and resentment.
- *We act out the anger in inappropriate ways.* Inappropriate expressions of anger include violence and outward aggression through verbal or physical attacks. Other inappropriate responses to anger include more subtle attacks against the person with whom one is angry. These attacks might take the form of gossip or put-downs or anything that undermines or hurts.[10]

It's okay for you and your child to feel angry but it's vitally important that we adults be good role models in showing children how to handle anger in healthy ways. Here are some anger-man-agement methods that will help you deal with your anger in non-destructive ways.

How to deal with the initial anger
- Stop! Back off.
- Take some deep breaths.
- Count to ten or twenty—slowly.
- Try to get away from the anger-producing situation and do one or more of the following.
  ° Call a supportive friend.
  ° Take a warm bath.
  ° Exercise—go for a walk or run.
  ° Lie down—read a book or magazine.
  ° Work in the garden or yard.

Once you've calmed down, think
- Strive for objectivity.
- Acknowledge and accept that you are angry.
- Consider the cause. Ask:
  ° Why am I angry?
  ° What is the situation that caused me to flare up?
  ° Did I feel threatened or afraid?
  ° Did I feel personally affronted?
  ° Was it an attack on my self-esteem or self-image?
  ° Am I afraid my child's behavior will make me look bad?
- Does the anger stem from a past hurt? Intense or inappro-priate anger may be rooted in past events. (Some coun-selors suggest that the more intense the anger, the more likely it is directly tied to a past trauma in your life.) If in-tense and/or inappropriate anger is a problem for you, con-sider seeing a counselor.
- Try looking at the situation from the other person's view-point.
- Consider the best course of action to take. Ask:
  ° Is there anything I can do to keep from responding angrily?

137

- ° Should I accept the situation or do something to change it?
- ° What are some possible resolutions to the problem?

Take Care of Yourself

As you probably know, it's *not* easy to consistently be a loving parent who disciplines effectively. To be successful, you must take care of yourself. Plan time in each day to relax. Give yourself time away from the children at least once a week. If you're married, arrange to spend time alone with your spouse. If single, maintain adult relationships.

Enjoy your children. Watch them play. Delight in the things they say and do. Learn to play with them. Although caring for children is a serious business, don't lose perspective. You need to have fun with them and enjoy them.

Know your limits and don't be afraid to ask for help. Parenting can be an exhausting job. Your children will seldom tell you what a terrific parent you are. Sometimes you wonder if you're doing anything right. When you maintain a relaxed and positive attitude and set reasonable boundaries, you will become more and more secure in your parenting skills and better able to cope with and care for your child.

13

PROTECTING CHILDREN
FROM ABUSE

Children have a right to be safe without being afraid. Children who have been taught to think for themselves are the safest children of all.

Sherryll Kerns Kraizer
The Safe Child Book

The world can be a dangerous place for children. A major concern for parents and caregivers is keeping children safe. How do we do that? How do we protect them? When children are small, adults must do their best to protect them. As they grow older and become more independent, abuse-proofing our children is more difficult.

Effective discipline must include training older children to take care of and protect themselves. In *The Safe Child Book* the author offers commonsense ideas for protecting children from abduction and sexual abuse. I strongly recommend that parents read this book or one like it so they can more fully prepare children for life in the sometimes cruel world.

Inform but Don't Frighten

We need to teach our children about the dangers in the world but we must do it carefully. We don't want to frighten them or tell them of dangers they are too young to grasp. We may be doing them more harm than good.

Kraizer tells us that children need to be informed of certain dangers if they are to keep themselves safe. We should not, however, resort to scare tactics. It is possible to "teach prevention of sexual abuse and abduction without fostering the idea that the world is an evil place in which the people your children love and trust the most might hurt them. It is possible to teach children safety rules using positive, reassuring techniques.... You've taught or will teach your children how to swim and how to cross the street without resorting to fear tactics. You didn't tell them horror stories about children who have been killed by careless drivers in order to ensure their safety on the streets."[1]

She suggests we instruct our children to avoid abuse by giving them some basic rules to follow. Kraizer goes on to list the best defenses our children have.[2]

1. A sense of their own power; [This of course is limited and must be reality based. Children are no match for adults either physically or mentally. To assume a child has power over an adult is to say the child could have prevented the abuse. This is simply not the case.]
2. The ability to accurately assess and handle a wide variety of situations;
3. Knowing where to get help;
4. Knowing they will be believed.

Preventive Tools

The "What If" Game

In *The Safe Child Book* the author introduces us to the "What If" game, designed to inform and at the same time challenge kids to think through problems and come up with workable solutions.[3] Kraizer uses this example of a mother and daughter playing the game in a supermarket. The mother is pushing the child in a shopping cart and gathering groceries.

Mother:	What if we were at the new shopping center together and you looked around and couldn't find me? What would you do?
Child:	I'd look for you and if I couldn't find you, I'd find a police officer and go to the police station.
Mother:	Could you go to the person at the first cash register you see and tell her you're lost?
Child:	I could go and say that my mom and dad are lost.
Mother:	Okay, so you'd go to the cash register and say you're lost. Could you do something else for me? Could you stay right in that spot and not move until I come to get you?
Child:	I'd stay right there.
Mother:	What if someone bothered you or tried to make you go with him?
Child:	I could hit and kick him.
Mother:	But he'd probably be bigger and stronger than you. There's something better you could do. What do you think it is?
Child:	I could SCREAM!
Mother:	Right! And who do you think would hear you if you screamed?
Child:	You would! Then I wouldn't be lost anymore, would I?

Role Playing

The "What If" game and versions of it are suggested in many books aimed at teaching children to protect themselves. One variation is the "What Would You Do If . . ." game. I found an illustration of this practical role-playing method in the book *Crimes of the 90s*.

Role playing involves setting the scene for situations that could happen to your child. Posing questions ("What would you do if . . .") places your child in a situation calling for his or her active participation of first recognizing a problem and then arriving at a solution.[4] An example might be, "What would you do if a car pulled up beside you and the driver asked you for directions?"

Remember, this is role play and parents should follow certain rules.[5]

- Don't paint vivid or specific scenes when posing "what if" questions. Make them vague and nonthreatening.
- While you can initiate the role play, encourage your child to ask most of the "what if" questions.
- Use role playing or acting as a way to make the game more fun and to firmly establish the expected behavior.
- Never respond to your child's questions by saying, "Oh, don't worry about that. That'll never happen to you."
- Be aware of age differences when role playing so older children aren't insulted or turned off and younger ones aren't confused or unnecessarily frightened.
- If a child asks the same questions repeatedly, you are probably not getting to the heart of his concerns. You may have to dig deeper into his feelings to discover what he actually wants to know.
- Help your child think through each situation step-by-step.
- Give suggestions when you feel the child has missed an important point.
- Repeat the role play from time to time as you would first aid or fire drill instructions.

"As your child learns to confront and deal with possible problems, he or she learns to deal with life on life's terms. Your child learns to live with the solution, not the problem."[6]

Leaving Kids Alone

Sometimes it is necessary to leave older children alone. In many families today with both Mom and Dad working, there are often circumstances when children are left alone. We call them latchkey kids. Perhaps it would be better if none of these kids had to stay home alone, but the fact is there are times when kids have to take care of themselves. The question isn't should I leave my child unsupervised at times, but when? Here is a checklist to help parents determine when kids are ready, along with a list of rules for the latchkey child.[7]

Is Your Child Ready for Self-Care?

1. Do you think your child is old enough to assume self-care responsibilities?	Yes	No
2. Do you consider your child mature enough to care for him/herself?	Yes	No
3. Has your child told you that he/she wants to try self-care?	Yes	No
4. Is your child a problem solver?	Yes	No
5. Is your child able to express him/herself clearly?	Yes	No
6. Is your child able to follow through and complete tasks?	Yes	No
7. Is your child comfortable staying alone?	Yes	No
8. Is your child comfortable entering your house alone?	Yes	No
9. Can your child lock and unlock the doors to your home without help?	Yes	No
10. Is there a neighbor that your child knows and can call in case of an emergency?	Yes	No
11. Do you have adequate household security?	Yes	No
12. Do you live in a safe neighborhood?	Yes	No

It is wise not to leave your child alone until you can answer yes to all of these questions. (Rules 9–11 may be helpful for families with more than one child.)

Commonsense Rules for Home-Alone Kids

1. Go straight home after school, soccer practice, music lesson, etc.
2. Phone Mom or Dad or contact a neighbor (as prearranged) immediately on arriving home.
3. When home alone, do not unlock doors or windows. Always speak to visitors from behind a locked door.
4. No one, not even a friend or a neighbor, is allowed in the house unless prior arrangements have been made with Mom and Dad.
5. When answering the phone or a door, never let anyone know you are home alone. Tell the caller that your parents are unable to come to the phone at that moment, then take a message.
6. When it gets dark, turn on the outside lights and as many inside lights as you need to feel safe.
7. If you have a dog or cat, keep it with you for company.
8. Know where to find important phone numbers. Call a parent or friend if you are frightened, confused, or have a problem.
9. No fighting ever! If you have disagreements, write them down for discussion with Mom and Dad at a later time.
10. Do the chores or responsibilities assigned to you.
11. Limit phone conversations to ten minutes.

Parents, make certain children know the rules and make it clear that they are expected to follow them. Let them know what you intend to do if they don't. If rules are broken, follow through with the consequences you've established.[8]

Protection from Sexual Assault

Talking to children about sexual assault may be very difficult for some parents, but in our world, where so many children are targets of sexual crimes, it is imperative that parents instill in their children some important principles. I would suggest you read several books that deal specifically with helping a child distinguish between the kind of touching that is okay and the kind that is not. A book I recommend is *With the Best of Intentions: The Child Sexual Abuse Prevention Movement.* The author, Neil Gilbert, challenges some of the prevention programs used by schools and counseling centers, warning that some so-called preventions may actually be harmful to children. According to an article by David Foster, critics of abuse prevention programs say:

> Programs have not been proven effective in preventing abuse and may confuse young children, possibly twisting their sexual development in later years. Even some advocates of prevention efforts say many programs now in use are misguided, outdated, and ineffective.[9]

This is a difficult area because, while we want to protect children, we do not want to rear a generation of fearful children, nor do we want to be so paranoid as adults we fail to allow our children to enjoy the warmth and comfort of others that can only come through touching. But we do need boundaries. We need to be aware of what our children are being taught and make certain they are not being damaged in the process.

As we delve into the problem of how to prepare children against assault, we are faced with a dilemma. Some experts say we should teach children to fight back, to say no. While saying no or fighting back may often be the best course of action, we must also be aware of the drawbacks. Saying no may aggravate the abuser and place the child in danger. One study found that "children with comprehensive training were more likely to be injured during abuse, possibly because they were more prone to fight back."[10]

The following list is one you may find helpful as you seek to educate your child about appropriate and inappropriate touching.[11]

- Your body belongs to you. You are special and unique. You are important and loved. You can take care of your body and you have the right to protect yourself.

- Your feelings are important. You can tell us how you feel anytime. We'd like to know if you feel worried, anxious, scared, or unhappy.

- You have a right to say whether or not someone touches you and how.

- Good touching makes you feel warm and happy. It's important to be hugged, patted, and squeezed.

- If someone touches you in a way you don't like, in a way that makes you feel funny or uncomfortable inside, or in a way that you think is wrong, it's okay to say no.

- If a person doesn't stop, you can say, "I'm going to tell," and then you tell, no matter what.

- If you're asked to keep a secret about being touched in a way that makes you feel uncomfortable, you say, "No, I'm going to tell." Not all secrets are bad. A good rule is: Good secrets make you feel good and happy. It's okay to keep good secrets. Bad secrets make you feel bad or uncomfortable. Never keep a bad secret.

- Other kids and adults do not have a right to touch the parts of your body that are private.

- We can make a list of people you can tell if someone tries to hurt you or touch the private parts of your body.

We've gone through a lot of suggestions on teaching children to keep themselves safe. Here's one more list of things parents can do to protect their children from sexual assault. Children must have guidelines, but it is the adults in the home and community who are ultimately responsible for preventing child abuse. Parents and caregivers can do the following.

- Pay careful attention to who is around your children. (Unwanted touching may come from someone you like and trust.)

- Back up a child's right to say no.
- Encourage communication by taking seriously what your children say.
- Take a second look at signals of potential danger.
- Refuse to leave your children in the company of those you do not trust or do not know.
- If the child is old enough to understand, include information about sexual assault when teaching about other safety measures.
- Remind children that even "nice" people sometimes do mean things.
- Urge children to tell you about anybody who causes them to be uncomfortable.
- Prepare children to deal with bribes and threats, as well as possible physical force.
- Teach children how to say no, ask for help, and control who touches them and how.
- Model self-protective and limit-setting behavior for your children.
- Monitor what your child is learning in school and from peers.

If a child has been sexually assaulted, you will need to do the following.[12]

- Listen carefully and try to understand what has happened from the child's point of view.
- Support the child for telling you by believing, being sympathetic, and not blaming or shaming. Let the child know he or she was not at fault.
- Try to determine what actually happened.
- Seek medical attention.
- Know local resources, and choose help carefully.
- Provide opportunities to talk about the assault.
- Provide opportunities for the family to talk, grieve, and go through a counseling/recovery process.

- Recognize that offenders do not change without appropriate intervention.
- With other adults in the neighborhood, organize programs to protect the children and support one another in the effort.
- Encourage and support educational programs designed to help communities understand, aid in protective efforts, and take affirmative action against all types of abuse.

An Abusive Society

When seeking to protect your child from abuse, you may want to consider some abuses children suffer because of unhealthy and at times immoral social conditions. Sometimes even programs and organizations designed to help children can end up hurting them.

"I like to think my husband and I are fairly good parents," Alicia, parent of three, told me. "We meet our children's needs. We nurture them. We take good care of them. My concern isn't so much that we'll damage our kids. I'm more worried about what's going to happen to them out there. Out in the world."

"What kinds of things worry you?" I asked.

"Schools . . ." she paused. "I worry about whether or not I should send them to public school. I hear so many things. Drugs. Kids taking guns to school. There's so much violence out there. My oldest starts kindergarten this fall. She's going to be exposed to so much."

"And you want to protect her."

Alicia nodded. "I suppose it's too soon to start worrying about this, but there's so much that's dangerous out there."

I can understand Alicia's concerns. Parents all over the country are facing similar fears. We've seen how children can be broken by abuse and neglect and even by a harsh word. Even more insidious are the ways in which children are damaged by people in power, who have little regard for the welfare of children. In the next few pages I'd like to cite a few examples of what I see as critical concerns that must be dealt with if we are to repair our damaged kids and keep them from being needlessly broken.

Schools That Damage Children

A serious issue confronting parents today is the public education system. Over and over I hear frustrated parents complain that their children are not getting a quality education. I personally know many wonderful teachers and school systems that work hard to meet each child's individual educational needs. Unfortunately public schools can be hazardous to a child's physical, emotional, and spiritual health.

Too Large and Impersonal

One concern voiced by a growing number of parents is that the schools are too large and, therefore, unable to adequately meet each child's unique educational needs. Many teachers complain that they have little time or energy for individual attention.

"In large schools," one parent said, "children are often given production-line status. As long as they conform and stay in line and do a mediocre job or better they're sent on through and at the end of the line they graduate. But if they are different, unique, challenging, or difficult, they may be sent on to another assembly line, which costs more to operate but is supposedly better equipped. Here they may or may not make the grade but they will learn one important lesson—they have been labeled defective by grown-ups, so it must be true."

One educator who chooses to home school said this: "Our children are guinea pigs in a system that has yet to find a way to properly teach children. We're continually changing things—it's the kids who suffer."

A Vote for Schools Is a Vote for Kids

Another parent told me she was upset about the way some school districts use the kids in their systems to promote the passing of levies and bonds for more funds. "I don't mind paying for my child's education, but most of the money goes for increased salaries and to sustain an inadequate and often failing system. I know I must sound bitter," she added, "but I resent it."

Even though statistics show that more money is not the answer to better schools, educators subtly inform children that people (often the children's parents and grandparents) who vote against these measures and increased taxes are actually voting against children.

Children are often asked to picket and carry propaganda to their families, and if the parent says no, the child may feel that the parent doesn't care or maybe doesn't even like kids. One grandparent voted against a school measure that would raise his taxes. His ten-year-old grandson, on learning of this, burst into tears. "Why, Grandpa," he cried, "don't you love me anymore?"

Undermining Parental Authority

Unfortunately, in some instances, the public education system has done much to wear down the fabric of the family. As one parent said, "I feel like the school is driving a wedge between parents and kids. They blame us when a kid goes wrong but at the same time they send the very strong message that parents don't know what they're talking about.

"We try to teach our kids our values, and the school goes against our beliefs. We finally took our kids out of public school and are home schooling. A lot of other parents are doing the same." She shook her head and added, "It's ironic, you know. We took our kids out of school because we felt the system was damaging to them. Now the school is accusing us of neglecting our kids by denying them the opportunity to socialize with other kids. That's insane."

In that same vein, a retired teacher said, "Just because some parents lack parenting skills, the National Education Association feels they must provide the children—all children—with what they need. Naturally the NEA determines those 'needs.'"

Unfortunately not all parents who voice concerns about the public educational system can afford a private school or feel they are able to home school. Only you can determine what's best for you and your family. The important thing is not so much what school your child attends, but your involvement in the process. Know who your child's teachers are and know the school's agenda. Voice your concerns. Be your child's advocate. Talk about injustices. Use problems as a springboard for teaching your child how to cope and how to deal with situations that arise.

Guns and Kids

There is much about our society that seems "insane." One of those insanities is violence, which I talked about earlier. Another of those insanities is the overabundance of guns. There seems to be unlimited access to firearms in our country. Whether or not firearms should be more strictly regulated continues to be a hot topic. This is not an issue of rights or government regulation. It is an issue of morality.

Innocent children die in firearm accidents every day. An increasing number of our children carry guns to school for protection and are using guns to settle disputes. Children are committing more violent crimes than ever before in our history. Even though there were twelve thousand handgun murders in 1992, firearm enthusiasts insist on maintaining their unrestricted right to bear arms.

According to columnist Don Williamson, "Americans are fifteen times more likely to be killed by gunfire than Europeans." While flaming public passion and promoting fear and the right to protect oneself, "the NRA actually caters to U.S. gun manufacturers who rake in more than $9 billion in annual sales while they crank out one gun every 20 seconds and 500 people a day are killed or seriously injured by their products."[13]

Not long ago I watched a presentation on one of the news programs about a child who killed a neighborhood boy in an accidental shooting. Even after the tragedy, the parents of the child who killed his friend said they would continue to keep guns in their home. It is, after all, their right.

One of a child's greatest needs is to feel safe. How can this happen when so many of our once quiet neighborhoods have become war zones?

Sexual Exploitation

Nearly every parent I talk with these days cites sexual issues as a primary concern. Are we telling too much too soon? Are we as a society sexually abusing our children? Are children being sexually harassed in the classroom? Is the promotion of sexual freedom subjecting children to ideas they are not yet ready to consider?

Child abuse laws help us understand what constitutes child sexual abuse. In appendix 2 you'll find guidelines for defining child abuse. I'd encourage you to read them before you read my commentary. As you do, keep the questions I just asked in mind.

Education or Abuse?

Sex education is being taught in nearly every public school system in the country. Many talk openly about sex and declare their sexual preferences to the world. While we do need to educate our children about sexual matters, we must take care that our teaching doesn't harm them.

Are children being taught the physiology of the human body, or are they being sexually exploited? Are they being prematurely exposed? They may learn the facts (how to do it), but are they being informed of the moral implications and ethical responsibilities involved?

Some health officials in this country now believe sex education and AIDS prevention should be taught to children as young as preschool, and some feel it ought to start in the cradle. In some schools condoms are being handed out to children as young as ten. When criticized for being overzealous, the "experts" tell us we must have them available just in case the child decides to have sex. Quite frankly, that makes about as much sense as giving the child the keys to a car, just in case he gets the urge to drive. Or making certain we have plenty of good quality drugs and sterile needles available in case a kid wants to shoot up.

Maybe I'm behind the times or maybe I'm zealous in wanting to protect children, but I find myself getting more and more angry. A TV commercial advocating "safe sex" showed an animated condom hopping out of a drawer and racing across the room. It hopped onto a bed and under the covers just in time. His assignment: Come to the rescue of a male and female about to have sex. Savior condoms? God help us.

As if that weren't enough, after the condom ad aired, some critics felt the ad didn't go far enough. They think kids need a demonstration of how to put on a condom.

The Threat of AIDS

Former Surgeon General C. Everett Koop once predicted, "The AIDS epidemic will soon change the behavior of everyone. When infected young people begin dying around us, others will be afraid to kiss anyone." Not quite. Dr. James Dobson, in a 1993 issue of *Focus on the Family* magazine, reported that "AIDS cases among teens and young adults grew 77 percent in the past two years." These kids are not afraid to kiss or to have sex. This seems to be borne out by the statistics Dobson quoted from *USA Today:*

- 69 percent of girls and 86 percent of boys have sex before age 20
- 3 million teens get a sexually transmitted disease yearly

Dr. Dobson then went on to say, ". . . the natural fear of the deadly HIV has been pacified by the safe sex nonsense." Dr. Joe McIlhaney, obstetrician and author of *Sexuality and Sexually Transmitted Diseases*, added this:

The Public announcements about "safe sex" infuriate me, because what they're saying is that you can safely have sex outside of marriage if you use condoms, and you don't have to worry about getting STD (sexually transmitted diseases). The message is a lie. The failure rate of condoms is extremely high, and that's why most married people don't use them.[14]

The obsession with sex in our society and the sexual emphasis in schools and in the media violate our children. Kids are being lied to and endangered. And the message may kill them.

Abortion Devalues All Children

The messages we send children are directly related to how much or how little we value them. Here are some facts from *Human Life News.*[15]

- 77 percent of the people polled in a 1991 Gallup poll believe that abortion "takes a human life."
- According to the *Los Angeles Times* in 1989, 57 percent of those polled considered abortion "murder."
- In 1991 the *Austin American Statesman* reported that 64 percent of Americans felt abortion should either be banned or limited to the "hard cases"—fewer than 5 percent of the total performed each year.

Despite the number of people who oppose abortion, it continues to be a legal method of dealing with unwanted pregnancies. Most of our courts advocate unrestricted abortion.

Most abortion supporters look at abortion from the pregnant woman's viewpoint—it is, after all, her body and should be her choice. Perhaps it's time to view the killing of an unborn child through the eyes of the children who survived pregnancy. How can a child feel valued when a human life can be eliminated like human waste? How can a child feel safe when his mother could have aborted him or his brother or sister? If children can be killed before they are born, then what prevents them from being maltreated after they are born?

Abortion breaks babies and rips apart the fabric of humankind.

Abusive Advertising

Another area of concern to many parents is advertising. Many businesses are exploiting children by aiming their advertisements at children.

Tobacco companies, though they deny it, target young audiences, enticing kids with "cool" characters like Joe Camel and his cronies. An ad may show clean, flowing streams, fresh mountain air, sexy women, and macho men. It tries to make smoking look so good. Why target kids? Propaganda has to start early so that by the time these vulnerable kids get into junior high, they are hooked.

Producers of alcohol show us that people who drink have lots of fun. The men are with-it studs. The women are sexy and they know how to make a man happy. And have you ever noticed how most of the beer commercials are broadcast during sports events? Will the children watching disregard the message? More likely, they will come away thinking alcoholic beverages will make them popular, strong, healthy, and physically fit.

Many toy manufacturers advocate greed. They brainwash our children by making the latest and greatest truck, doll, or gadget irresistible. Children who don't get these wonder toys may feel deprived, and Mom and Dad become the bad guys for not giving in to their children's desires.

Advertisers who present adults as ignorant slobs who can't tie their shoes without the kid's help are not only showing contempt, but are being negligent. Children need to know the adults in their lives are strong, intelligent, and competent enough to take care of them and keep them safe. They do not need the burden of feeling they must care for adults.

These are only a few examples of concerns parents have voiced. I'm sure you could easily add to the list.

What Can We Do?

My goal in discussing these matters is to promote dialogue, uncover wrongs, and discover what changes we can make to assure a better future for our children. It is to bring us face-to-face with some of the problems of today's children and parents and work at finding solutions.

We must voice our opinions and concerns, write to our congressmen, call in complaints, write books and articles, and refuse to purchase offensive materials. Many of you are already doing that. But we need to press on, keep to the task, and not let up until we feel that our society has become a safe place for our children.

We may not be able to resolve all the wrongs we see but we can make certain our voice is heard. We may not be able to rescue and protect all the children in the world but we can try to save those within our reach. Our most important tools will be a willingness to get involved, determination, knowledge, empathy, and love.

14

HELPING CHILDREN HELP THEMSELVES

Adults who care for children must be adequately prepared for the task. This doesn't mean we all have to have degrees in psychology. Knowledge is a good thing and it certainly doesn't hurt to have read some good parenting books and magazines. But being prepared means getting in touch with the child we used to be so that we can better think like children and empathize with them. We need to have our imagination primed, our intuition fine-tuned, and our eyes and ears open.

We must approach children, not with an attitude of "I am a grown-up. I will fix you," but with an open and humble heart that says, "I love you and accept you and your feelings. I want to help. With your imagination, my experience, and God's guidance, maybe we can find a way."

When working toward helping children find solutions to their problems, you must keep an open mind. Approach children anticipating what they're going to teach you about themselves and the way they see the world.

Each child is unique, with a different set of life experiences. Each comes equipped with a personality and differing abilities to assimilate information and adapt to situations. And each can help you discover what needs to happen to bring him or her healing and happiness.

Be a Counselor

Those who have the most success in caring for children are usually those who have taken time to learn about them and to form a warm and caring relationship with each one. In a sense, you need to be a counselor to the children you care for. The best counselors set aside a portion of time during which they give individuals their undivided attention, work to develop a relationship, and look for the most effective method of helping those individuals help themselves.

Let's take a look at some things that happen naturally in our bodies and minds that help us cope. Then I'll identify ways we can help children regain and use those abilities in healthy ways.

Staying Balanced

Our bodies have magnificent built-in mechanisms designed to help us maintain our equilibrium or sense of balance. In the physical sense, when one part of the body is impaired, other parts work harder to compensate. People who have lost one of their senses, such as hearing or sight, find that the other senses usually compensate by becoming more highly developed.

My grandson Jonathan began having seizures a couple of days after birth as a result of low blood sugar and his body's inability to metabolize fat in the normal way. The doctor explained that seizures increase blood sugar levels and that Jonathan's body was trying to compensate and to maintain the right balance to survive.

Just as our bodies struggle to maintain equilibrium, so too do our minds and spirits. If something happens to disturb the balance, our bodies will adjust and readjust to set things right, or at least to compensate for the differences. Our minds do the same thing. Flexibility is vital to our survival. The struggle to stay in balance is evident at an early age when, as children, we begin to compensate for wrongs done to us. How well we are able to do that depends on our level of resilience or our ability to cope.

When we are hurt or become anxious, our built-in defenses or coping mechanisms spring into action. The moment life goes wrong, consciously or subconsciously, we set out to make it right.

We use a number of defense mechanisms to keep ourselves emotionally balanced and fine-tuned, to keep our emotional and spiritual selves from falling apart. Let me give you an example. Attorney and therapist Lynne Finney revealed that at age forty she underwent hypnotherapy for numerous mental and physical problems. During the course of therapy she found that she could not remember anything about the first eleven years of her childhood. Further treatment sessions revealed a macabre past. She had been sexually abused and tortured by her father from ages four through eight. Finney's first reaction was denial. She felt she was going crazy. Eventually she was able to face the trauma and work through it.

Today Finney works with adults who were abused as children and has written a book, *Reach for the Rainbow.* "Our minds are incredible," Finney says. "They protect us from what we are unable to bear."

Here are some of the defense mechanisms we use to protect ourselves.

- *Repression*—We force unpleasant or unbearable thoughts or memories into the unconscious. Sometimes an act of violence against us is so unbearable, we dismiss it as a thing that couldn't have happened.
- *Denial*—We refuse to accept a given situation.
- *Projection*—We project unacceptable thoughts, desires, and impulses onto others, thus setting them outside of ourselves so that responsibility can be shifted. It is easier to attack someone else than to engage in an internal battle.
- *Rationalization*—We devise plausible and acceptable explanations for our situation or actions. It usually involves deceiving oneself.
- *Sublimation*—We express or divert unacceptable impulses and negative energy, such as inappropriate sexual desires, anxiety, anger, and fear, into safe and acceptable channels.[1]

159

Defense mechanisms can make us more resilient and increase our ability to cope, enabling us to handle even the most difficult problems. Unfortunately few of us react in truly healthy ways and our defenses may, as Willard Frick, a professor and practicing psychotherapist, says, "become disruptive and self-defeating. In general, defense mechanisms distort reality and may give us inaccurate perceptions and inappropriate behavior. Thus, if certain defenses become habitual and dominant in our lives, they may inhibit personal growth."[2]

Helping Children Cope

One of our jobs as caregivers is to help children cope with wrong or unfair circumstances by guiding them to work out their hurts and disappointments in healthy ways.

Seven-year-old Travis has just been taken away from his abusive parents. Because his parents are drug addicts and have been unable to care for themselves or him, Travis has learned how to take care of them as well as himself. He has taken on the parent role.

Children Services has just pulled him out of a deplorable situation. His parents were arrested on drug charges and the police found Travis alone in a small, run-down apartment. He'd been rescued from squalid conditions, yet Travis is angry. He lashes out at his foster parents, calls them names, and fights with everyone who looks at him.

You'd think Travis would be grateful that someone intervened. Instead, all he talks about is going home. Travis has been forcibly removed from the only home and parents he's ever known. He is probably feeling all the emotions that come with a tragic and abrupt loss: denial, anger, guilt, and remorse.

At the same time, he may be feeling relief at finally being free of the drug-induced rages and the senseless beatings he endured. Part of him may feel guilty for feeling relieved. All in all he is a storm of emotions and doesn't know how to control them. They rage inside of him. Sometimes they lash out like streaks of lightning and growling thunder. Other times they simmer inside, leaving him sullen and despondent.

His equilibrium has been thrown off balance at all levels. His defenses are likely saying, *Do whatever you have to do to get back to where you were. It may not be good but it's what you know.*

In chapter 12 I suggested that we look beyond the behavior. That's especially important when we're dealing with kids who carry the pain of childhood abuse and neglect. How can we help Travis? We can't allow him to go home. We don't want to give up on him. Sadly, the child welfare system is full of children whose behavior is so disruptive no one wants them.

I'd like to offer some suggestions for helping kids like Travis learn how to deal with their emotions and cope with their very real and present crises. One of the first areas of concern for us in caring for broken children is in helping them deal with losses.

Time to Grieve

Kids like Travis need to be given whatever time they need to work through the grieving process and to adjust to the new life. Even though the relationship Travis had with his parents was unhealthy, he loves them, and his relationship with them didn't stop simply because he no longer lives with them. It isn't easy to change a lifetime of patterns and beliefs.

Travis lost his parents, his home, and a lifestyle he'd grown accustomed to. As I stated in my book, *The Humpty Dumpty Syndrome:*

Most professionals who work in the mental health and medical fields are well aware of the grief process and the importance of grief work in coping with losses. Yet most patients and clients resist or at least want to hurry grief along. In both my personal and professional experience I've found that grief will have its place whether we want it to or not. If we suppress it, our tangled emotions will build and become gnarled clumps of anger, rage, guilt, shame, or depression. These emotional by-products, if not properly managed, can cause severe mental, physical, and even spiritual damage.[3]

Chad and Paula recently lost their infant to SIDS. To spare their six-year-old daughter, Jasmine, they told her as little as possible. Chad and Paula went to grief counseling but they didn't take Jasmine. They talked to each other about their feelings but they didn't talk to their little girl.

Jasmine became increasingly ill-tempered, whiny, and depressed. The couple's grief counselor suggested that Jasmine's behavior might be a reaction to unresolved grief.

"But she's so young," Paula said. "I just don't want her to be hurt."

"She's already hurt," the counselor replied. "Jasmine needs to work through her grief as much as you do."

By working with Jasmine and encouraging her to talk about her baby brother's death, the counselor discovered that Jasmine's behavior stemmed from the fact that she blamed herself for the tragedy. "I told God I didn't want him," Jasmine confessed. The child was convinced that God had taken the baby back and that her mom and dad didn't like her anymore because of what she'd done.

Jasmine's parents had inadvertently reinforced her beliefs by telling her the baby was in heaven with God, by leaving her with a sitter when they went to the funeral, and by not including Jasmine in their grief work. Her parents had no idea how Jasmine felt, because they didn't think to ask.

As people who care about kids, we tend to want to protect our children and shelter them from the hard knocks life delivers. But we can't. In fact in disallowing their contact with uncomfortable, sad, or painful circumstances, we may end up hurting them. The very methods we use to protect them may add to their confusion and prolong their pain.

Sorting through Feelings

Children don't necessarily need to get in touch with and name everything they're feeling. Most of them probably couldn't if they wanted to. But we'll want to give them permission to feel what they feel and to openly express those feelings without fear of reprisal. Then we can help them choose one or two of the biggest problem areas and work on solutions.

How do we help children when life's crushing realities invade their homes? One way is to encourage them to express their emotions in healthy ways.

Mandy pushed her two-year-old brother, Zach, aside and grabbed her doll out of his hands. He screamed.

"Mandy," Jeannette shouted, "you know better than that. Give Zach the doll and say you're sorry."

"Mommy, no!" Mandy broke into tears and ran to her room. "It's my doll."

Jeannette helped Zach settle down and gave him another toy. Whenever her husband's job took him out of town, Mandy became incorrigible.

Jeannette squared her shoulders and prepared for battle. "Mandy, I have had it with you. Stop crying this instant and give me that doll." The moment the words left her mouth she kicked herself for being so insensitive. She knew that Mandy wasn't deliberately making trouble. She was acting out her feelings.

Jeannette pulled the child onto her lap, brushed her dark hair aside, and kissed Mandy's forehead. "I'm sorry for shouting at you, sweetheart. Pushing Zach was wrong, but I think I understand. You miss your daddy, don't you?"

Mandy sniffed and nodded. A fresh batch of tears rolled down her cheeks. "And I miss Peaches too."

Peaches, Mandy's puppy, had been hit by a car and killed several months before. Jeannette and Ted, not wanting her to be upset, quickly replaced Peaches with another puppy. In their eagerness to avoid traumatizing their little girl, they neglected her need to work through her feelings.

I've used Mandy as an illustration because even though she hasn't been abused in the same sense as Travis, the same principles can apply to all children who are struggling with feelings they may not understand or be able to express.

Accept Emotions as Normal

We often categorize feelings as negative or positive as if some were right and others wrong. Consequently we may feel guilty for experiencing feelings such as despair, frustration, or anger. Feelings are neither good nor bad; they simply are. When normal emotions are suppressed, they don't go away but reappear in more severe forms, such as depression or inappropriate behavior. When we accept, express, and deal with emotions, they are less likely to lead to serious and wrongful acts.

In our eagerness to protect and correct our children, we often inhibit them. We may punish them when they are angry, or try to tickle them out of their sadness. It upsets us to see children unhappy. Some parents and caregivers see a child's unhappiness as a reflection on their ability to parent well. An inner voice tells them that if they were doing their job, their kids would be living happily ever after.

Have you ever comforted a tearful child by saying, "There, there sweetheart, don't cry." Instead of trying to talk a child out of being sad, empathize. Hold him close and say something like, "You seem to be feeling very sad. Can I hold you until you feel better?" or "You look angry. I wonder what could have upset you?"

Acknowledge emotions and help children express them. Emotions are God-given mechanisms that help us cope with difficulty in our lives. When we stop our children from feeling what they feel, we inhibit them from being who they are.

Unfortunately children, especially younger ones, are not always able to talk about their problems. Sometimes they're not even sure what's troubling them. Even children who have a good command of language skills may have difficulty describing what's wrong. Here are several avenues for exploring feelings with children.

Show by Example

When you are honest about how you feel, you not only open the door for further communication, you show your children healthy ways to express themselves as well. Use phrases such as

"I feel sad when . . . ," "I feel frustrated about . . . ," or "I feel angry right now because . . ."

Venting feelings is a healthy way to deal with life situations. Occasionally, however, the venting can lead to destructive and unacceptable behavior. Sometimes our emotions build like water behind a dam. The dam may burst and send emotions flooding outside of established boundaries. As we allow children to express their feelings, we also show them how to manage them by example and through loving discipline.

Perhaps your child is letting all those emotions out by throwing a tantrum or whining. Instead of running away from home, try the advice of Dr. Lawrence Kutner of Harvard University Medical School. He wrote an article called "How to Un-whine Your Child."[4] One of his suggestions is to break the cycle by whining together. You do this in a lighthearted way so as not to mock or belittle the child's feelings.

For example, your child starts complaining and whining the moment you pick him up from day care. You might say something like, "Sounds like you had a rough day. I did too. I think I'll whine with you." Then take turns moaning and groaning and giggling. I've done this in the past and it really works. You do end up laughing and feeling better—more objective.

Parenting is hard work and a big responsibility, but try to retain a sense of humor. One of the best ways to defuse family conflicts is to find something to laugh about. Children love to laugh.

Name Those Feelings

When you sense a child is having difficulty expressing himself, help him. You may say something like, "It sounds like you're *angry*" or "I wonder if you're feeling *jealous* about my holding the new baby" or "You seem *happy* today." Do this with all kinds of feelings, happy as well as sad, contemplative as well as angry.

You may also play a charades type of game I call "Name Those Feelings," where players take turns pretending to be angry, sad, happy, afraid, worried, and so on, and the others guess what the emotion is.

Draw Them Out

Children may not always be able to express their concerns, fears, or feelings directly, but they can draw, tell stories, and play. Drawing, painting, and working with clay can provide opportunities for children to vent their pent-up emotions in healthy ways. Working with these various art forms can also provide caregivers with a door to the child's inner self.

Drawing gave ten-year-old Jeffrey an opportunity to express concerns and fears he had kept tucked away for more than a year. He drew a picture of a sandy beach and an ocean. On the beach he'd drawn his mother and sister and his mother's new boyfriend. He drew himself swimming in the water. Swimming beneath him was a shark with long pointed teeth. When Jeffrey had finished, I asked him to tell me about the picture. He explained that the man on the beach was trying to protect his mom and sister but couldn't because he didn't understand that the real danger was in the water. "Only I can protect them from him." Jeffrey pointed to the shark, heaved a great sigh, and then added, "and I'm not sure I'm strong enough."

I sat there stunned. In his drawing Jeffrey had opened himself up to me. He'd exposed his need to take care of his mom and sister now that his father was gone. Even though there was a new man in his mother's life, Jeffrey still felt responsible. He also let me know he felt weak and inadequate to do the job.

We can help children deal with trauma by telling stories about other children who have had similar experiences. Children love stories, and we're fortunate to have some exceptional books that deal with loss, loneliness, divorce, abuse, and the like.

Another way children express their feelings is through play. Be alert to how children play and what they play with. Listen to what they say. To really get the full benefit from play, get down on the floor and enter into the game. It takes time, but you can learn so much.

I've used a tool I call the "Animal Game." It might go something like this: "If you were an animal today, what would you be?"

"A tiger. Roar!"

"Why would you want to be a tiger?"

"So I could be mean and big."

"And if you were a tiger, what would you do?"

"I would bite off Jathan's hand."

"Oh, that would hurt. The tiger would have to be awfully mad to bite your little brother. I wonder what he's mad about."

Well, you get the idea. Enter into the role play. Don't push for explanations or lecture the child on what he should or shouldn't be thinking or feeling, but listen and learn. Identify and empathize with how he is feeling. That may be all the child needs. Once you've done that, you can start thinking about how to channel the actions that accompany the feelings, such as anger, into more appropriate expressions than biting or hitting. By using your imagination, you can encourage children to express what they feel and playact those feelings in a safe place.

A Time for Silence

I used to think that every statement uttered in my presence needed a response. I felt duty bound to add my opinions or advice to every conversation. I have learned over the years, however, that some things don't require our comments. Some things just need to be heard. This principle became clear to me one night early in my nursing career. Among my patients was a cancer patient. He was only forty-nine and he needed to talk.

I stopped at Tom's bed during rounds. He seemed restless. "Are you okay?" I asked.

"Would you be?" he challenged.

"Probably not. Do you need anything for pain?"

He nodded.

"I'll be back as soon as I can." I quickly checked the other patients, then hurried back to the nurse's station to draw up his pain medication. My mind and stomach churned. I knew Tom needed more than something to ease his pain. He needed to talk and I didn't have any answers.

After I'd given Tom his injection, he said, "Could you sit here awhile? I won't be able to sleep and I could use some company. Dying gets sorta lonely."

I swallowed hard, blinking back the tears, and then with learned composure said, "Sure."

"You drew night shift this week."

I nodded.

"I . . ." his voice broke. "I'm gonna die. I don't mind so much for myself—yes, I do. But my wife and the kids. What are they going to do without me?"

I couldn't answer. I never could cry and talk at the same time. I touched his shoulder, hoping to offer some comfort. He reached up and took my hand in his. Tom talked for a long time. After a while he released my hand and said, "Thanks for staying. You helped me a lot."

"But," I stammered, "I didn't say anything."

"You listened."

I had listened. Tom hadn't needed a long dissertation on letting his feelings out. He hadn't needed me to tell him how terrible it was that he had cancer or how God was in control. He hadn't needed me to lecture him on keeping a stiff upper lip. He had only needed someone to listen. Sometimes that's all our children need as well.

Empowerment

Some of our best solutions for dealing with problems will come from the children—all you need to do is listen and learn. While I was interning for my master's degree in counseling, one of my young clients and I were working on a way to overcome a major obstacle in his life—anger. Paul was an eight-year-old boy who'd been the victim of violence at the hands of an out-of-control father. Despite his efforts, Paul couldn't seem to work within the guidelines of an anger management program we were trying.

One day when Paul came to see me, he excitedly told me he'd learned how to draw a maze at school that day and asked if I wanted to see one. I nodded. He drew a maze on the blackboard then asked me if I could find a way out. I did—eventually, then used his enthusiasm for mazes to do a little experiment. I drew a maze and in it put two obstacles—a deep lake and a bear. "In order to get through the maze," I said, "you have to figure out how to get past these."

Paul grinned and said, "That's easy, I can take a boat across the lake."

"What if you don't have a boat?" I asked.

Paul thought for a moment, then said, "I'll float across on a log."

When he got to the bear, he gave a deep sigh. Resting an elbow on his knee, he cupped his chin and stared into the air. After a minute or two of thinking, his eyes lit up. "I know. I'll throw a rock in the tree, make him look up, and run past him."

"That might work." I gave him a hug. "You're very good at this." At his suggestion, I drew another maze on the blackboard. "What if we put the Anger Monster in this one," I suggested. "I wonder if we can figure out a way for you to get past it." (We had previously given the anger a separate identity to help him deal with it in an objective manner. We had determined that every time he hurt someone in anger the monster got bigger, and every time he used his anger management skills to avert physical violence, it got smaller.)

Paul grinned and said, "I'll make him littler and littler." The next week Paul reported that the Anger Monster was half the size he'd been before.

In playing the maze game, Paul was able to come up with a plan to solve his own problem. He was learning that no matter what the odds, there is a way out. He was also learning that he had the power within himself to find solutions to many of life's problems.

Scripture assures us that we can do all things in Christ who strengthens us (see Philippians 4:13). God empowers us to do much more than we ever dream possible. We in turn have the ability to empower others.

One of the most positive approaches we can use with abused or damaged children is to empower them to cope with life's obstacles so they can make significant changes in their lives. Empowerment comes as we work through specific problems with a positive, yet honest, approach to finding solutions and methods of coping. We do well to take the apostle Paul's advice in Philippians 4:8 and think about what is good, right, positive, and possible, rather than dwelling on what is wrong and impossible. This approach works well as long as we use it to help us deal with problems, and not simply as a defense to help us avoid pain or to convince ourselves that problems don't exist. When we focus on what we can do, we are motivated and empowered to develop tools to cope with and overcome whatever difficulties arise.

For example, ten-year-old Robbie couldn't sleep at night. His father had abused him, and in a counseling session Robbie said, "I dreamed that my dad came into my room through the window and killed me. He could do it for real."

After empathizing with his fears, I said, "I wonder what could protect you so you wouldn't have to be afraid any more."

Robbie thought for a moment. His eyes widened and a smile emerged. "A dragon! If I had a dragon outside my room he'd make sure I was safe."

"Could you have a dragon?"

"Sure, he's in my imagination. He's mean and a hundred feet high."

"Oh, he sounds scary."

"He is, but don't worry," Robbie assured me. "He won't hurt you cause you helped make him."

Robbie had no trouble sleeping in his room after that. He had used an energy within himself to fight the nightmare as well as a very real threat. To an adult, this may seem like a childish game, but for Robbie a guard dragon was exactly what he needed at the time.

Resolutions can present themselves in many ways and in many forms, but that won't happen unless you're willing to set aside time for the problems to reveal themselves and for solutions to appear. I know that sounds a little strange, but when your main tool is the child's imagination, you can't just place an order and expect it to appear.

A Secret Weapon

Sometimes what we do to help our children works. Sometimes it doesn't. Sometimes children emerge from their troubled lives as mature, well-balanced, resilient, emotionally healthy adults. Sometimes they don't. As sad as it may seem, we can only go so far in our guidance, encouragement, praise, discipline, and compassion. Our efforts though will be made stronger and more effective if, at all times and in all places, we use our secret weapon—prayer.

We have a silent partner who cares more about our children than we do. All the good in us as parents and caregivers finds its source in God. There may be times when you wonder if you'll make it through, but be assured God will provide a way.

In my own struggles as a parent, there were times I wanted to give up and times I cried myself to sleep wondering if I'd ever get it right—if my children would survive. Then I would remember God, my loving, nurturing parent who would hold me to his breast and comfort me. In my mind I would climb onto his lap and give myself over to his care.

We can do a great deal to bring our Jacks and Jills to a safer place. We can nurture them, love them, and even help them help themselves, but is that enough? Before I bring this book on healing broken children to a close, I feel we must take yet another step—that of creating a safe and supportive community.

Part Four

CREATING A SAFE COMMUNITY

The village raises the child.

Old African Saying

15

WORKING TOGETHER

Have you ever heard the sayings, "There is safety in numbers" and "A threefold cord is not quickly broken"? When we work together we can accomplish so much more than when we try to make it on our own. In the same way, children can be more easily put together and child abuse can be greatly diminished if we work together as a caring community.

As members of a caring community we offer children and parents support by recognizing, defining, and reporting child abuse, and, of course, preventing abuse through intervention.

The first thing we need to do as people who care about the welfare of children is to recognize and understand the depth and proportions of child abuse. Dr. Kempe, a pediatrician, was given credit in 1962 for helping doctors recognize the physical symptoms of child abuse. He coined the term "battered baby syndrome" (which is discussed in more detail in appendix 2) and identified six stages of awareness that people experience in developing an understanding of the child abuse issue.[1]

1. Denial that abuse is significant or widespread and a belief that it is only carried out by drug-crazed parents.
2. The community begins to take note of the more brutal forms of abuse, such as battering.
3. The recognition of more subtle forms of abuse such as neglect and failure to thrive.

4. The recognition of emotional neglect and abuse, and concern about effects of rejection and scapegoating of children by parents [and others].
5. The slow and painful recognition of the existence of sexual abuse.
6. The belief that every child has the right to be wanted and to receive proper food, health care, and loving attention.

Dealing with Denial

Child abuse, like death, draws responses of denial and anger. Our psyches have a difficult time accepting the fact of abuse. A hurt child is an assault to our very nature. Some say the abuse is not as bad as the media make it seem.

Millions of adults today close their ears to the truth because they are frightened by it and because it may stir in them memories of their own childhood that they'd rather not remember.

Author and psychotherapist Alice Miller writes:

It requires a considerable act of the imagination for us to conceive of the situation of a small child, totally exposed to the willfulness and, not infrequently, the madness of adults. This madness can quite readily coexist with a polished sociability on the part of the parents [and others], so that it remains completely invisible.

These adults can be well-respected pillars of their community on one level, but on another, more personal level may "take out the repressed torture of their own childhoods on their children." They may be seen as good, kind, caring people, yet . . . remain completely blind to their children's needs because they learned as [youngsters] that a child's needs do not count. As they never received protection, loving care, orientation, or tenderness from their own [parents], they had to suppress the accompanying needs. As a result, they remain blind to their own children's needs, unless positive experiences in their personal relationships have allowed this blindness to heal.[2]

Repression and denial are often found in adults who were abused as children. Again quoting Alice Miller, "The reality of adult cruelty is so beyond [our] comprehension that the child is in a state of constant denial in order to survive." As adults, they continue to repress by making the parent right and heaping the blame on themselves. They forget "how it was for that small child to live side by side with two omniscient, stern, and unpredictable parents."[3]

I was not abused as a child, yet my career in nursing and counseling brought me face-to-face with the reality of it. Still, in all honesty, I found it difficult to accept the startling truths about child abuse and neglect. I procrastinated many months in researching and writing this book. I didn't want to be reminded that such cruelty exists.

As I read and heard story after story of damaged children, I at times wished I could hand the task over to someone else. It broke my heart to have to delve so deeply into so painful a topic. Perhaps the hardest part of all was to admit that as a member of my community I am at least partially responsible for the abuse that occurs. If I fail to act, I too am guilty. As the old saying goes, "If we are not part of the solution, we are part of the problem."

In the end, I couldn't walk away. I had to force myself to face the issue head on. In the process I went through Dr. Kempe's stages. I found there were still issues I needed to resolve. One was denial. Even though my ears and eyes witnessed abuse, I didn't want to believe it was actually as widespread as the statistics seemed to indicate.

When I heard that one in four females would be raped or sexually abused before the age of eighteen, I thought, *That's impossible.* Then when I discovered it was happening in my circle of family and friends the statistics took on a harsh reality. Eventually I cut through my veil of denial and moved into resignation, then anger, and with that, grief.

Grieving for Broken Children

Dr. Kempe's list for recognizing child abuse reminds me of the stages of grief: denial, anger, isolation, bargaining, depression, and acceptance or resignation.

Child abuse, whether it happened to us as children or is happening to our own children or grandchildren or a neighbor, is something we will eventually need to grieve over. Abuse is a shocking and terrible tragedy that wounds children—injuring and at times even destroying innocence and human dignity. It places human beings created in God's image in the category of animals . . . or worse.

You may need to work through the stages until you can accept abuse as a tragic reality. You may find yourself struggling with a history of abuse in your own childhood. If the process becomes too difficult or painful for you, consider seeing a counselor to help you through the trauma.

Author Joanne Smith says, "Grief is the process of putting back together the pieces of a broken heart—a hole so deep in the middle of your heart that it aches and hurts and you think it will never stop."[4]

To create a safe community for children, we must first recognize that abuse is a very real and present danger to every child. We must learn to recognize the signs of true child abuse and know what is abuse and what isn't.

Defining Child Abuse

An important factor in preventing child abuse is having a working knowledge of child abuse laws. This, as you'll soon see, is not easy.

Many assume that since child abuse and neglect are against the law, somewhere there are statutes that make clear distinctions between what is and what is not child abuse or neglect. But this is not the case. Nowhere are there clear-cut definitions of what is encompassed by the terms.[5]

Still it is important that we try to gain as clear an understanding as possible of child abuse laws and issues if we are to be informed and effective parents and caregivers.

According to the federal *Child Abuse Prevention and Treatment Act of 1974 (PL 93–237)*, child abuse or maltreatment is:

The physical or mental injury, sexual abuse, negligent treatment, or maltreatment of a child under the age of eighteen by a person who is responsible for the child's welfare under circumstances which would indicate that the child's health or welfare is harmed or threatened thereby.

Since the definitions tend to be vague, you'll need to consider several factors in determining whether or not a child has been or is being abused. The following questions can help you clarify whether or not abuse has actually taken place as you consider each factor.

- *The degree of abuse.* How serious is it? How many signs of abuse does the child show?
- *The consistency of the abuse.* Does the abuse happen routinely and is it of the same type?
- *The frequency of the abuse.* Does it happen often?
- *Overall attitude of the parent toward the child.* Is the parent generally loving? indifferent? angry? negligent?
- *Consensus of opinion.* Is it just my opinion that abuse has occurred? Am I being fair? Does my community/culture agree?
- *The demeanor of the child.* How is the child acting? Does he fit the profile of an abused child?

I recently visited a friend who was caring for a darling little four year old named Matthew. When I greeted him, he ducked his head and closed his eyes, shrinking as though he expected me to hurt him. I knew he had been abused even before his caregiver told me. His mother's boyfriend had forced Matthew to keep his head down

179

for long periods and had locked him in closets for punishment. My heart ached for this little boy and I wanted to gather him in my arms and tell him no one would hurt him anymore. Unfortunately that was not to be. The boy's mother ignored warnings from her family and went back into the abusive situation, taking her children with her.

In some cases we may easily recognize abuse. At other times we may be uncertain. Appendix 2 gives guidelines and signs for determining whether or not a child is being abused.

Reporting Child Abuse

One of our obligations as members of a community that cares about children is to report cases of abuse to a child welfare agency. Reporting abuse, however, is not a responsibility to be taken lightly. In appendix 3 you will find a detailed explanation of the reporting process.

Why You Should Report

Child welfare agencies strongly urge individuals to make reports, saying, "You should report any reasonable suspicion of abuse; you do not have to prove it. If you suspect a child has been abused, phone your local Children Services office to discuss your concerns with a caseworker."[6] There are basically two reasons for intervention. It can avert more serious abuses and it can help parents attain the skills they need to take better care of their children. By reporting abuse you may be instrumental in:

- stopping the abuse
- getting help for the family
- helping the family understand how serious the problem is

Some professionals are subject to mandatory reporting laws, which require that they report any suspected abuse. Mandatory reporters include physicians, dentists, school employees, nurses, social workers, day care workers, clergy, law enforcement officers, psychologists, eye doctors, chiropractors, foster care providers, attorneys, naturopaths, professional counselors and therapists, firefighters, and emergency medical technicians. These people must report suspected abuse or face a maximum penalty of one thousand dollars and thirty days in jail. They may also be sued in civil court and risk losing their professional certification for failing to report.

The Reporting Dilemma

I have personally reported several child abuse cases. Child abuse hotlines provide an excellent way for a concerned friend, family member, or neighbor to remain anonymous and still provide help to the child who is in serious danger. While I support reporting when a child is in clear and imminent danger, I also have some deep concerns about the practice of reporting.

While reporting might sound like a simple solution, arbitrarily phoning in suspected abuse is not always in the best interest of the child or the family. Reporting an abuse may save a child's life. It may, on the other hand, cause serious damage to children and their parents. As a caring community we need to be aware of both sides of the issue.

Unfortunately some irresponsible people have misused hotlines as a means of retaliating or for the malicious reporting of abuse that does not exist. In one case, a father accused his wife of sexually abusing their two-year-old daughter so he could gain custody of the child. Even though medical evidence and psychological evaluations supported the mother's claim of innocence (she was never arrested or charged), she couldn't get her child back. Words had stained her character and nothing she did or said could erase that stain. "After all," even those who supported her maintained, "if the words were said, there might be some truth in them."

In another case, Maggie, a day care manager, reported the mother of a child she cared for because she had noticed a number of unexplained bruises on the child's body. A few days later, the mother accused Maggie's husband of sexually abusing her child and accused Maggie of covering it up by naming her as the abuser.

These people and thousands of others across the United States and Canada are victims of child abuse laws—reporting gone awry.

What if we report an incident of what we think is abuse and it isn't? What if a social worker snatches a child away from the parents on a reporter's say-so and subjects that child to even more severe trauma? What if the doctor jumps to conclusions or acts on his suspicions rather than waiting for test results? It happens.

Victims of Child Abuse Laws

A national organization called VOCAL—Victims of Child Abuse Laws—offers assistance and support to people who have been falsely accused of child molestation and abuse. VOCAL has more than one hundred chapters and several thousand members nationwide. These individuals have been caught up in a bureaucratic system fueled by what many call "child abuse hysteria."

Author Mary Pride in her book, *The Child Abuse Industry,* states that even as early as 1985 more than one million North American families were falsely accused of child abuse.[7] "In the U.S.A. alone, 1,024,178 families were hotlined in 1984. Of this number 58 percent were unsubstantiated. Of the remainder, less than 10 percent involved anything serious enough to deserve the title 'child abuse.'"[8]

More currently, a booklet issued by the Children Services Department in Oregon states that in 1989 there were 25,018 reports made to CSD or law enforcement agencies in Oregon. After screening and assessing these referrals, 11,047 separate incidents of child abuse were confirmed. Of those, 8,674 children were actually listed as "abused."[9] One can't help but wonder what happened to those who were eventually found innocent. How much trauma was done before the parents were cleared?

It is important here to point out that although Pride makes some valid points, she tends to relate experiences with CSD in a mostly negative light. I personally know of several cases where CSD workers went into a home to check out a report of abuse, then worked with the parents to correct what actually turned out to be more parental ineptness than abuse. These parents and their children were actually better off for the intervention.

Pride insists that the government agencies designed to protect the rights of children have gone too far. Social workers can pull a child from the home "without showing any evidence (other than an anonymous hotline call) for why the children should be removed."[10]

Further, people who report abuses can remain anonymous and as long as the report was made "in good faith" are immune to lawsuits or prosecution. Individuals who are falsely accused have little recourse against persons who falsely accuse them.

Once the child is removed from the home the parent must prove, often through expensive litigation, that they are fit. Even then, they are under probation. As one parent said, "You are guilty until proven innocent and it's up to you to prove that you have never done any of the things social workers object to."[11]

A Flawed System

In addition to making mistakes in taking children from non-abusive parents, social workers, in attempts to keep families together, have sent children back to parents who hurt, maim, and sometimes kill their children.

I recall the story of Gregory, who died at the age of two. At three months of age, Gregory had been placed in foster care after his parents had brought him to the hospital with a broken arm, brain injuries, bruises, and an injury to his left leg. His foster parents gave him a warm loving home and Gregory eventually lost the terrified look he'd get when someone moved him. He learned to crawl and laugh. Gregory was safe and loved.

He was eighteen months old when the state decided to send Gregory back to his parents for a second chance. The foster parents protested, fearing Gregory would suffer abuse again if returned to his natural parents. Social workers, however, felt the parents should have the opportunity to try again.

Less than a month later, Gregory's father killed him. The child's father was sentenced to seven years and one month in prison. How could it have happened? A look at the records would have shown that the boy's father had been arrested only two months earlier for beating Gregory's mother.[12]

To create a safe community, we must work together in a cohesive effort to more closely watch the system.

Lisa's Story

Author Joyce Johnson, in her book *What Lisa Knew*, tells the story of Lisa Steinberg and of the tragic mistake on the part of the community and the system designed to protect children.

At the age of six, Lisa Steinberg weighed forty-three pounds. She was a little thinner than most other first-graders. She had big hazel eyes and red hair. If she had ever grown up, people would have called her an Irish beauty. The fine shoulder-length hair hadn't been shampooed for a long time; it was terribly tangled and matted. It hid a large red bruise on the right temple that would be discovered in the emergency room at the hospital, along with two other large fresh bruises on her jaw and the back of her head. . . .

When the blanket was lifted off the child under the white lights of the pediatric emergency room, the cops and the medics saw all the other bruises. Elizabeth Steinberg's small body was a map of pain. It seemed as if she had been hit just about everywhere—on her arms and the calves of her legs, on her chest, her buttocks. One of the biggest bruises was in the center of her lower back—not a place where a child would be likely to injure herself. There were fresh scratches on her elbows, as if someone had grabbed her there. Her parents had just let her go dirty—her feet and ankles had a crust of black grime. The hair and the feet shocked everyone almost as much as the bruises.[13]

When I first heard about Lisa, I wondered how a child could have suffered so much without anyone knowing. I later discovered in various writings that several people had called police on numerous occasions to report screams and loud noises. Police would come to investigate and would find evidence of spousal abuse but couldn't make an arrest because Hedda Nussbaum, Lisa's mother, refused to file a complaint against Joel Steinberg.

About ten days before Lisa's death, a tollbooth operator saw Lisa in the backseat of the car, bruised and sobbing. He reported what he'd seen. Steinberg made excuses, saying she had a stiff neck, and again, no charges were made.

We will never know about all the horrors Lisa endured but she did leave a small piece of her painful existence behind. As Johnson explained, the police found drawings on a sketch pad under the couch. With a black crayon, Lisa labeled one of her pictures "Mommy." In this picture, Hedda Nussbaum has a face with no features; orange hair flames out from around a blank circle. A large portion of this drawing has dense crayon scribbles over it. Maybe after Lisa finished, she was afraid she'd revealed too much. Still you can see one of Hedda's arms thrusting forward very plainly. A large, thick, forceful arm. The hand at the end of it bristles with sharply pointed fingers.

The drawing marked "Daddy" on the facing page has even heavier crayoning over it. Nothing is left of Joel Steinberg except two enormous, obliquely slanted, ovoid black eyes.

Elsewhere, usually in the very lightest pencil, Lisa Steinberg drew herself. A tiny, freckle-faced ghost, a girl without arms.

On the first two pages of the pad is a story about a little animal. It was lost in a dark wood. "It krad and krad."

Lisa Steinberg was a child lost in a dark wood.[14]

Why didn't someone stop it? Lisa's torturous life and eventual death could have been prevented if more people had gotten involved and if someone had asked the right questions, probed a little deeper, and recognized the symptoms. The legal system failed Lisa, but we as a society must take the blame as well.

Responsible Reporting

The fact that our system for dealing with and preventing child abuse is flawed does not mean that we should stop reporting. Under no circumstances should we withhold crucial information that might save a child's life.

If we are to be child advocates, we need to be aware of what constitutes abuse and know when to report and when to get involved. We must be responsible in our reporting, but if we strongly suspect that a child may be the victim of abuse, we should file a report with a child welfare or law enforcement agency. For more information or advice before filing a report, call Children Services or seek counsel from a qualified professional.

Child abuse is a very real and very present problem that happens with alarming frequency. Responsible reporting of suspected child abuse can help not only the children, but the parents as well. Every child deserves to be protected against abuse. As child advocates, we can help in many ways. Recognizing, defining, and reporting abuse are steps in the right direction.

Our best help, however, will come in the form of intervention—that is being a community that reaches out to parents who have abused or are in danger of abusing their children. In chapter 4 I talked about high-risk parents and their need for support, guidance, and encouragement. We as a community can give that support and encouragement.

16

THE SUPPORTIVE COMMUNITY

In a deeply honest book, sharing her own painful struggles as an abusive mother, Kathy Miller writes, "I felt depressed and helpless, as if I were riding a raft down a coursing river without oars or a rope. And my distress calls to God seemed to be unheard."

She tells of a visit to a friend. They watched a news report about a child abuse case and the parent's arrest. Kathy writes:

My heart started beating hard and I took a deep breath.

"You know, Jill, sometimes I understand how parents might be tempted to mistreat their children. Kids sure can make parents angry." Laughing nervously, I looked at her and hesitantly waited for her reaction.

"Well I sure can't," she retorted, shaking her head. "These people are awful. They ought to be arrested."

I jerked my head away, hot tears stinging my eyes. *Lord, am I really that bad? Doesn't anyone else get angry like I do?*[1]

Kathy desperately needed someone to confide in, but telling her secret could destroy her life—her family. She feared that if she came forward and confessed, authorities could take her children away and she could go to jail. And worse, her secret would be out and everyone would know that she had abused her children.

In an act of supreme courage, Kathy finally admitted she needed help, asked for it, and has since turned her life around. She was able to make the transition from abusive parent, to a parent who, though not perfect, is able to adequately and appropriately care for her children. For Kathy and many other parents who have hurt their children or who feel they might, the answer lies not in hiding the truth, but in being honest, open, and vulnerable.

In many cases those who abuse children want to find a way out. They often carry inside them a dark and shameful secret and are terrified someone will discover it. As a society we don't make it easy for them to come forward. In fact with so much attention now being paid to the issue of child abuse, we may be pushing some parents even deeper into their guilt-ridden closets.

We can help parents and others in a number of ways. One way is to report the abuse and hope the offender and the child are able to get the help they need. Another way is to become more personally involved in family support systems in your community.

Be Informed

If you are to become a child advocate and intend to intervene to help children and their parents, it's important that you know what is available in your community in terms of parenting classes, support groups, community services, day care facilities, and child welfare agencies.

For example, did you know that *The Adoption Assistance and Child Welfare Act of 1980* requires states to offer support services to families before removing a child from the home? If a child must be taken from his or her natural parents and placed in foster care, a specific plan for the child's care and welfare must be in place and reviewed every six months. Of the 250,000 children placed in foster care each year, more than half are eventually reunited with their families.[2]

Find out if there are any public and private agencies that work with parents and children at risk. One private agency, Homebuilders in Washington, works with about five hundred families a year. According to one report, in 95 percent of the families who received treatment, domestic violence decreased. Of these families 85 percent reported improved communication skills among family members.[3]

Parents Anonymous

A group parents can turn to for help is Parents Anonymous. With more than twelve hundred chapters in the United States, Parents Anonymous is a support group of people with similar problems getting together to offer one another support and encouragement as well as specific ways in which to get the help they need. In PA parents can receive personal help from experienced parents and not have to deal with government agencies with their red tape and long waiting lines. As in Alcoholics Anonymous, parents can be part of the group without fear of being judged or condemned. Members are encouraged to ask for help—to phone another member and talk out their feelings rather than venting their frustrations on their children.

While investigating the help that is available, you may notice some areas of need in your community. For example, while quality day care is available for people who have money, the poor cannot always take advantage of these services. Nearly every mother needs a break from her children on occasion, but to the financially handicapped parent, this may be impossible. Add to that the bureaucratic maze of government agencies and you may find that we are indeed extremely short of appropriate and available help to low-income parents. We need more agencies who will open their doors to parents in need.

Church and Community Involvement

In many baptismal services, the congregation pledges support and promises to see that the child is properly reared. The church family agrees to oversee the care of their children. Yet we rarely see these promises carried out in the reality of day-to-day life.

Adults in a "church family" become their children's aunts and uncles and grandparents. What would happen if these "family members" offered to babysit occasionally, or came by to chat, offer assistance—maybe even did a few household chores for the overburdened mother?

I'd like to see more churches and volunteer agencies offer drop-in day care centers for parents in need of a few hours of rest. In lieu of payment, parents could volunteer to work several hours a week. They would be able to get out now and then plus learn parenting skills from qualified day care facilitators.

Many hospital maternity wards provide rooming-in (where baby stays in the hospital room with Mom) and many now offer parenting classes. But how about providing a visiting nurse or volunteer "grandmother" to make regular visits and provide on-the-job training to new parents for the first few months so that new parents can have support and learn parenting and coping skills all at the same time.

This same type of support could be offered to parents with older children who haven't had the opportunity to be trained in effective parenting. The service could offer assistance for as long as the parent needs it. This might be especially helpful in families who have a difficult-to-manage child or a handicapped child.

Perhaps churches or counseling centers could provide a lay counselor (trained volunteer) for every family with a new baby in the congregation as well as to families in crisis or in highly stressful situations. This type of hands-on help fosters accountability on the part of the parent.

While we're encouraging parent education, why not begin by teaching junior high and high schoolers, both male and female, what it is really like to have children? We teach sex education; why not go the rest of the way and let them know about the aftermath of falling in love and having sex—the baby? Some schools already do this. The students "adopt" an egg or other fragile item that they have to treat like a baby for a period of time.

One young single mother, who began dreaming about having a precious bundle of joy with her boyfriend, is now teaching other young women what motherhood is really like. Her dream turned into a nightmare of hemorrhoids, morning sickness, hours of painful labor, postpartum depression, and lots of dirty diapers. She says, "If someone my own age would have shown me what it's really like, I probably would have waited."[4]

Preventive Programs

Every community needs programs geared to help parents who were themselves abused as children. Many of these parents want and need help to break the abuse cycle and learn how to care for their children in loving, nurturing ways, rather than by resorting to violence.

I recently read about a program in Oregon called Exchange Club Child Abuse Prevention Program where trained parents go into the home of parents who need help and support in caring for their children. The volunteer or parent aide spends five hours a week (during two days) for a year, working with the parent(s) to build their self-esteem and enable them to become better parents. The volunteer also teaches child development and shows the parents how to discipline their children in nonviolent ways.

The exchange director was quoted as saying, "This is not a Band-Aid. This is getting in and changing how people think, believe, and behave."

Personal intervention through programs like these can assure better treatment of children, but only to the extent that they have enough trained volunteers available. As of this writing the exchange club had only twenty volunteers with ten more in training, hardly enough to deal with thousands of abused children in the state.

Family Involvement

There are times when a problem can seem overwhelming—when all you hear about is how terrible life is and how hopeless

191

it all seems. Then you read an article that is like a silver lining on a dark, cloudy day. Bill Carey, administrator of the Children Services Department in Oregon, wrote about an innovative approach to strengthening and preserving families. He tells of an unmarried couple whose child was removed from their home. CSD called the couple's extended family and arranged what they call a "family unity" meeting. Fifteen family members showed up. According to Carey:

> Family members wrote a plan. The unmarried couple separated. A family member volunteered to chaperone the father's visits. And the couple agreed to counseling. Family members challenged the couple to talk about marriage, and an uncle agreed to take the baby's father to AA meetings.

By respecting the family and utilizing their strengths, caseworkers helped put a broken family back together again. "Our focus," says Carey, "is on strengthening families, not removing children and putting them in foster care."

It's wonderful to hear about success, and perhaps the greatest success of all is this. "Over the past four years, Oregon's emphasis on family preservation has resulted in out-of-home care being *reduced* by 1.3 percent. By contrast, the national *increase* has been 33 percent."

Carey ends his report by saying, ". . . we're now acknowledging that family members and people who care about them can strengthen and preserve families in ways that no government agency can."[5]

As you try to provide a supportive, caring community, you may occasionally run across what you feel is a hopeless case and the only hope for the child is removal from the abuser. This is the exception. Most parents want to be caring and responsible. They want to be able to cope with problems that arise and develop parenting skills that will allow them to enjoy their children. Most child care professionals agree that children are better served if the family can stay together. The good news in all of this is that about 90 percent of abuse is treatable. Education of parents is the key.

Community Minded

Our society needs to become more community minded. We don't all need to run for political office, create more laws, serve on the town council, organize more task forces and agencies, and join protest marches, but we must become more communal in spirit.

We might do well to spend time getting to know one another. We need less isolation and more of the "small town" atmosphere where people know what's happening in one another's lives. We need to become more relational on all levels.

How will all of this help children? One of the factors contributing to the abuse of children is the way we have evolved from a community-oriented lifestyle, where people worked and played together and did what was best for the social structure as a whole, to the individual or egocentric lifestyle, where each person works to achieve what he perceives is best for himself. The egocentrism or "island" mentality prevalent in our society promotes greed and selfishness with little concern for how our behavior affects others.

Too much privacy combined with the lack of community can be dangerous for children because they are often left unnoticed by outsiders, as author Joyce Johnson points out:

The privacy of American families is sacrosanct. It has far more legal protection than the lives of children. With each hour, new infant citizens are born, and there's no way of knowing, of really determining, what fates they're born into. The birth is recorded; the mother and baby leave the hospital; the child drops out of public view, vanishes behind the locked door of the home. As Dr. Richard Krugman, a child-abuse specialist, points out, the state doesn't officially hear of the majority of these children again until five or six years later, at the time they start school. Then it becomes possible to track them to a certain extent.

> Birth, then, is like a lottery. Babies win, babies lose. In this country, we do not even question this awesome randomness. We accept it as the inescapable order of things.[6]

While maintaining a certain amount of privacy is important, it is not always in the best interest of parents or children.

If we are to make a difference for the children of tomorrow, then we need to open our doors and allow others access to our family affairs. We must be willing to pour ourselves and our love beyond the boundaries of our fortresses and well-built fences out into the streets and houses and apartments and slums where broken children live.

Oswald Chambers says:

> If human love does not carry [us] beyond [ourselves] it is not love. If love is always discreet, always wise, always sensible and calculating, never carried beyond itself, it is not love at all. It may be warmth of feeling, but it has not the true nature of love in it.[7]

Caring for any child is a wonderful opportunity and an awesome responsibility. The way our children turn out is a reflection of the adults who care for them. We have a lot of work to do in our homes, churches, schools, and communities to make the world a place where children can feel safe and well cared for. Let's continue to work together to make a difference.

APPENDIX 1

NURTURING SKILLS ASSESSMENT

For each question, circle the number under the answer you have chosen. Answer each question as honestly and objectively as you can.

	Yes	No
1. Do you prepare or oversee the preparation of meals?	1	0
2. Do you provide foods from the four basic food groups every day?	1	0
3. Do you frequently offer your child water during the day?	1	0
4. Are you concerned about feeding your child a balanced diet?	1	0
5. Do you usually offer meals at a fixed time each day?	1	0
6. Do you sometimes leave your child with a child under age twelve or a person otherwise unable to provide adequate care?	0	1
7. Do you ever leave your young child or children alone in the house?	0	1
8. Does your child get at least nine hours of sleep most nights?	1	0
9. Do you set a routine bedtime for your child and adhere to it most evenings?	1	0
10. Do you take your child in for routine dental examinations?	1	0

* Adapted from questionnaire originally published in "Assessing Adequacy of Child Caring: An Urban Scale," *Child Welfare* 57, no. 7 (1978): 439–49.

11. Do you make certain your child's teeth are brushed two to three times a day?	1	0
12. Do you take your child's temperature when he or she is sick?	1	0
13. Do you (or others) smoke near or around your child?	0	1
14. Do you verbalize and enforce safety rules such as "No playing in the street"?	1	0
15. Do you apply sunscreen to your child when he or she is playing in the sun?	1	0
16. Have you taught your child his or her address and phone number?	1	0
17. Do you plan for and celebrate special occasions?	1	0
18. Do you generally dress your child in clean, pressed, color-coordinated clothing?	1	0
19. Do you regularly check your child's wardrobe and replace worn-out and outgrown garments?	1	0
20. Do you regularly replace buttons and snaps and mend your child's clothing?	1	0
21. Do you encourage your child to wash hands before meals and after using the toilet?	1	0
22. Do you keep medications, cleaning agents, insecticides, and other potentially toxic substances locked away and out of your child's reach?	1	0
23. Do you make certain your child is clean and well groomed, both at home and away?	1	0
24. Do you feel it is important to keep your home relatively clean and neat?	1	0
25. Do you plan occasional overnight trips and vacations for your family?	1	0
26. Do you and your child visit museums, zoos, fairs, and historical or cultural areas together?	1	0
27. Do you spend time alone with each child?	1	0
28. Do you read to your child several times a week?	1	0
29. Do you exercise (walk, run, play games) with your child at least once a day?	1	0
30. Are prayers said at most meals?	1	0

31. Do you offer comfort when your child is upset?	1	0
32. Are prayers said at bedtime?	1	0
33. Do you often cuddle or relax together—especially at bedtime?	1	0
34. Do you take pictures of your child and enjoy reminiscing about fun experiences?	1	0
35. Are books and magazines available in your home?	1	0
36. Do you enjoy talking with your child?	1	0
37. Do you follow through on offering rewards?	1	0
38. Is your child often ignored when he or she tries to tell you something or ask questions?	0	1
39. Is your child ever ignored when he or she comes to you for a hug or to be held?	0	1
40. Do you often feel you can't get your child to mind?	0	1
41. Are you consistent in your discipline methods?	1	0
42. Do you ever threaten punishment by the use of scare tactics?	0	1
43. Do you ever spank with an object (e.g., switch, belt, stick)?	0	1
44. Do you often find yourself ignoring unacceptable behavior in your child?	0	1
45. Do you often yell at your child?	0	1
46. Do you allow your child to make messes?	1	0
47. Do you see your child as a burden?	0	1
48. Does your child have a designated play area?	1	0
49. Do you monitor what your child sees on television or in the movies?	1	0
50. Are you careful of the language your child is exposed to?	1	0
51. Do you allow your child to make choices?	1	0
52. Do you provide opportunities and supplies for your child to draw, color, paint, and sculpt?	1	0
53. Do you provide age-appropriate toys and books for your child?	1	0
54. Do you encourage your child to care for and pick up toys?	1	0

55. Do you assign age-appropriate "jobs"?	1	0
56. Do you proudly display your child's artwork in a prominent place in your home?	1	0
57. Are you teaching your child to respect the property of others?	1	0
58. Are you actively involved in your child's education?	1	0
59. Do you allow your child to openly express feelings?	1	0
60. Are you teaching your child to be respectful of adults?	1	0
61. Do you set aside a "quiet time" each day for napping, reading, or just being silent?	1	0
62. Have you taken your child fishing?	1	0
63. Have you planted flowers together?	1	0
64. Have you flown a kite together?	1	0
65. Do you and your child sing together?	1	0
66. Do you encourage your child to laugh and joke with you?	1	0
67. Do you teach your child to care for the environment?	1	0
68. Are you teaching your child values—to discern right from wrong?	1	0
69. Do you believe you are a good role model for your child?	1	0
70. Do you encourage your child to express his or her feelings?	1	0
Total	__	__

When you have completed the questionnaire, count the numbers you have circled and add the two columns together. The higher your score, the higher your nurturing ability. (The highest possible score is 70.)

Appendix 2

Defining Child Abuse

The following pages give definitions and symptoms of child abuse that can help you determine whether or not a child is actually suffering abuse.

Child abuse includes any of the following.[1]

- *Physical abuse or battering*—deliberately inflicting pain that may result in bruises, welts, burns, cuts, broken bones, sprains, bites, poisoning, etc.
- *Psychological or emotional abuse*—a continuing pattern in which a child is ignored, rejected, terrorized, isolated, or corrupted and which results in *serious* emotional damage to the child.
- *Neglect*—when a child's health and safety are at risk because a caregiver fails to provide food, shelter, or medicine and to meet other basic needs. (Bear in mind that many living in poverty have little choice in what they can provide. The abuser in such cases may be the one who has plenty, sees the need, but criticizes rather than gives aid.)
- *Threat of harm*—threatening actions or written or verbal statements that cause a child to believe he or she is in danger of being abused. (There must be a substantial risk of harm, placing the child in clear and present danger.)
- *Sexual abuse or exploitation*—the use of a child for adult sexual stimulation or gratification, including but not limited to fondling, rape, and child pornography.

Several medical conditions may result from child abuse. Among these are failure to thrive (FTT), battered baby or child syndrome, whiplash shaken infant syndrome, and Munchausen syndrome by proxy (MSP).

Failure to Thrive

Failure to thrive, or growth retardation, is a diagnosis given to children who do not grow and develop within what experts term normal guidelines. Growth retardation can be the result of either physical or emotional neglect. Abused children are often smaller than other children the same age.

It is very important, however, that we don't automatically assume that a child's failure to thrive is abuse related. FTT can easily be misused as a basis for falsely accusing parents of abuse. In fact FTT may reflect a number of physiological problems, including allergies, an immature digestive tract, or a metabolic disorder that hinders the body's ability to properly utilize food. Even the smallest of children may be within the normal limits when family history is considered.

Battered Child Syndrome

Battered baby or child syndrome is a pattern of physical abuse characterized by multiple injuries, permanent injury, and sometimes death. Although the syndrome can occur in a child of any age, the victim is most often three or younger. Although Lisa Steinberg was six, she matched the criteria of a battered child (see page 184). The criteria are as follows.

1. When examined, doctors find clear evidence of previous injury. Lisa had numerous bruises and had clearly been neglected.
2. The child may suffer battering at the hands of both parents. Or one parent may batter while the other is a passive witness, perhaps a victim of abuse as well. Lisa may have been battered by both parents. Evidence indicated that her mother had been a battered wife.

3. Parents may not bring the child in for treatment until the child is seriously injured or near death. In Lisa's case, the mother called 911 reporting that Lisa had stopped breathing.
4. Parents of a battered child will often claim ignorance as to how the injuries occurred or give bogus explanations. There is generally a wide discrepancy between the clinical findings and the parents' story. Lisa's parents claimed she'd gotten sick after eating vegetables and that she'd been vomiting. The father gave no explanation for the multiple bruises, particularly the one on her forehead. Vomiting did not account for the blood in the back of her eyes or her deep coma.

Whiplash Shaken Infant Syndrome

Shaking infants and small children may cause severe damage to the brain or spinal cord. Children may die as a result of these injuries. Whiplash shaken infant syndrome is caused by holding the child by the arms or trunk and shaking him. The child may suffer blood clots around the brain, hemorrhaging of the retina (blood behind the eye), bone fractures, brain injury, and bruising—particularly on the arms, legs, and chest.

Munchausen Syndrome by Proxy

This particular form of abuse is rare, but it has received attention of late because of a case presented on a national television news program. Munchausen syndrome is a condition of adults who falsify or exaggerate medical histories, make up symptoms, and subject themselves to needless medical intervention and even surgery. In Munchausen syndrome by proxy, the abusing parent may induce or fake symptoms of illness in his or her child, subjecting the child to unnecessary medical procedures, tests, and hospitalization. The MSP parent brings the child in repeatedly for medical care. Interestingly, the reported symptoms subside when the child is separated from the parent.

Signs of Abuse

Physically and emotionally abused children may exhibit various symptoms, including the following. (Please note that these signs may, but do not necessarily, constitute abuse.)

- Unmet physical and emotional needs
- Lack of medical attention
- Dirty clothing, body odor, unkempt appearance
- Inappropriate clothing—long sleeves in warm weather; light clothing or no jacket or coat in cold weather
- Repeated incidence of unexplained injuries
- Burns or bruises, especially more than once
- Coming to school early and leaving late or not wanting to leave
- Seeming overly tired
- Failing to grow normally
- Being left alone unsupervised at too young an age (Note that with both parents in a family working outside the home, many children are latchkey kids but are not necessarily being neglected or abused. The age of the child would be relevant here.)
- Engaging in violent or dangerous behavior
- Talking about beatings
- Seeming overly anxious and eager to cooperate
- Seeming secretive or withdrawn
- Showing an abnormal need for emotional support, always searching for favors and help
- Suddenly losing interest in school or experiencing a drop in grades
- Difficulty sleeping, nightmares
- Running away

In the case of sexual abuse, the child may show these signs in addition to any of the symptoms listed above.

- Interest in, knowledge of, or acting out sexual behaviors inappropriate for the child's age (For example, one mother I talked with was distraught when she caught a three-year-old neighbor child teaching her children how to "play sex" by using oral stimulation of the genitals. Oral sex should not be part of a three-year-old child's experience.)
- Physical symptoms, such as difficulty walking or sitting, genital pain, pelvic inflammation, bleeding, or underclothing that has been torn or stained
- A compulsive need to be clean
- Seeming overly ashamed or uncomfortable about sexual topics or normal activities, such as undressing and showering in a gym class with members of the same sex
- A sudden change in behavior, personality, or relationships—the child may seem withdrawn or disinterested in formerly enjoyable activities, may be unable to concentrate, and may experience a drop in grades
- A sudden dislike of a particular person, activity, or place; not wanting to go somewhere or do something that was formerly a routine or pleasant activity

The last two signs suggest that some kind of sexual abuse has recently taken place, creating the sudden change in behavior. For example, Nicole used to spend hours at the neighbor's house. Quite suddenly the visits stopped. Nicole continually made up excuses not to go. On investigation, Nicole's mother discovered that the man who lived next door had fondled Nicole.

Children often blame themselves for the abuse or may feel powerless because they can't stop it. In addition, all types of abuse may be evidenced by poor grades, problems with drugs or alcohol, suicidal thoughts and actions, and eating disorders (compulsive eating and obesity; bulimia—eating and then forcing yourself to throw up—or anorexia—eating so little that you endanger your health). The child who has been sexually molested may try to stop the abuse by making herself look unattractive or by hurting herself.

In abuse of any kind we may see isolation—a lack of close friends, not wanting to invite friends home, or not wanting to talk about parents. The child or teenager may seem depressed and hopeless about life and the future.

Many of these signs by themselves do not indicate serious abuse, but when there is a combination or a consistent pattern of symptoms, it should serve as a warning.

A Word of Caution

When we consider what constitutes child abuse, we'll need to be particularly wary about the category of abuse tagged as "emotional." The guidelines defining emotional abuse and neglect are often vague and subjective. They leave much room for misinterpretation.

Many children do, in fact, suffer emotional abuse and neglect. Unfortunately this type of abuse can be extremely difficult to identify, as can the cause of the problem.

It would be criminal to report parents or caregivers for suspected abuse because the child seems withdrawn or acts out angrily, when the abuser could actually be another child or group of children who tease him because of his size, his name, or his clothes. The one responsible for the child's distress could also be a teacher who belittles him. Perhaps the child suffers from low self-esteem because he's unable to do something other kids in his class can do, such as jump rope.

Before making accusations, we must as much as possible get the whole picture. We need to ask ourselves, *How is the child acting? Is he or she showing signs of abuse?*

All children deserve the opportunity to grow up in a loving home where they can feel secure and well cared for. We can help them achieve that by recognizing abuse and reporting abuse when it is appropriate to do so.

Appendix 3

Guidelines for Reporting Child Abuse

Child welfare agencies have been put in place primarily to protect children and assist families in assuring child safety. According to *A Guide for Mandatory Reporters of Child Abuse,* in Oregon every report goes through a process that includes six possible decision points.

1. *Screening.* All reports are screened through an extensive information-gathering process to determine if abuse has occurred, if there is any risk to the child, and if an immediate response is required. Trained, experienced workers determine from the information they receive whether or not to intervene. Screening may also include interviewing the child, parent, family members, and other persons involved in the child's care.
2. *Assessment.* If actual abuse is suspected, a caseworker assesses the family situation by gathering more detailed information.
3. *Determination.* The caseworker then determines whether abuse has occurred and whether the child is at risk of further abuse.
4. *Decision.* If the caseworker determines that abuse has occurred, he or she decides whether the child can be safely left in the home.
5. *Provision of services.* The caseworker assesses the family system to see what services will be of the most benefit to

the family and then draws up a plan for providing those services.

6. *Case closure.* When agency personnel feel that their services are no longer needed to maintain the child's safety, the case is closed.

Before calling in a report, you'll want as much information as possible. *What You Can Do about Child Abuse* says:

If possible, we would like to know the names and addresses of the child and parent; the child's age; the type and extent of abuse, as well as any previous evidence of abuse; the explanation given for the abuse; and any other information which will help establish the cause of abuse or identify the abuser.[1]

The amount of information you receive will, of course, depend on your relationship with the child and the parents.

When a Child Confides in You

There may be times when, in the process of your caregiving, a child will confide in you. This can put you in a difficult situation. Do you report on the child's say-so? How do you question a child without putting words in his mouth?

Research now shows that children are extremely susceptible to suggestion. It has been shown that in the past some counselors were able to encourage children to admit to abuse that did not happen.

In their book *Do You Have a Secret?* authors Pamela Russell and Beth Stone provide a guide for adults on how to interview a child who may have been sexually abused. Their advice will work well in any abuse situation. If a child confides in you, do the following.

- Believe the child. [Children generally do not lie about abuse. They can, however, confuse reality and fantasy and be influenced by adults whom they want to please. To a child, sto-

206

ries can be as real as life.] Your belief in them can help them feel that someone is on their side.

- Be warm and supportive.
- Talk in private and in his or her own vocabulary.
- Affirm the rightness of telling the secret.
- Emphasize that the child is not responsible for the act or situation.
- Avoid focusing on the abuser.
- Never condemn the abuser to the child.
- Report the situation immediately to a child welfare agency.[2]

Getting Follow-up Information

If and when you report an abuse, you may want to know what happens in the case. Unless you are professionally involved, caseworkers can't reveal confidential information concerning the case. They may be able to tell you whether or not your report was founded. You may be able to obtain the necessary information to help the child in the future.

Appendix 4

Sources of Help

For more information on treating and preventing child abuse contact:

Child Abuse Listening Mediation
P.O. Box 718
Santa Barbara, CA 93102
(805) 682-1366

Child Welfare League of America
440 1st St., N.W.
Washington, DC 20001
(202) 638-2952

Childhelp USA/International
6463 Independence Avenue
Woodland Hills, CA 91370
(818) 347-7280

Children's Rights of America
12551 Indian Rocks Road
Suite 11
Largo, FL 33544
(813) 593-0090

Clearing House for Child Abuse
P.O. Box 1182
Washington, DC 20013

Institute for the Community as
Extended Family
P.O. Box 952
San Jose, CA 95108

International Society for Prevention of Child Abuse and Neglect
1205 Oneida Street
Denver, CO 80220
(303) 321-3963

National Committee for the
Prevention of Child Abuse and
Neglect
332 S. Michigan Avenue
Suite 1250
Chicago, IL 60604-4357
(312) 663-3520

National Exchange Club Foundation for the Prevention of
Child Abuse
3050 Central Avenue
Toledo, OH 43606

Parents Anonymous
675 W. Foothills Blvd.
Suite 220

Claremont, CA 91711-3416
(909) 621-6184

Pro-Family Groups:

Eagle Forum
Box 618
Alton, IL 62002

Focus on the Family
P.O. Box 35500
Colorado Springs, CO 80935-3550

Missouri Parents and Children
Box 16866
Clayton, MO 63105

Pro-Family Forum
P.O. Box 8907
Fort Worth, TX 76112

VOCAL
(Victims of Child Abuse Laws)
P.O. Box 8536
Minneapolis, MN 55408

National Association of State VOCAL Organization (NASVO)
P.O. Box 621314
Orangevale, CA 95662

NOTES

Chapter 1: *It Shouldn't Hurt to Be a Kid*

1. "Vision of Girl in Window Haunts Neighbors," *The Vancouver (Wash.) Columbian*, 15 November 1993.

2. *S.O.S. America! A Children's Defense Budget* (Children's Defense Fund, 1990), 6.

3. Sylvia Ann Hewlett, "America Fails Its Children Publicly, Privately," *Oregonian*, 9 July 1991, sec. B, p. 7.

4. James Willwerth says in "Hello? I'm Home Alone . . . ," *Time* (March 1, 1993), 46, that recent figures estimate that ten million latchkey kids are left at home alone for the afternoon—or longer—virtually every weekday. (This observation is not meant to criticize those parents who find it necessary to leave their children alone for short periods of time, but to increase our awareness of and concern for children left alone.)

5. Hillary Clinton, *It Takes a Village: And Other Lessons Children Teach Us* (New York: Simon and Schuster, 1996), 11.

6. Clark County Sheriff's Association, *Crimes of the 90s: Crimes against Children* (Walnut Creek, Calif.: Stuart Bradley Productions, 1991), 109.

7. Lisa Levitt Ryckman, "Mom Loses Two-year-old to Stigma over Nursing," *The Oregonian*, 4 February 1992, sec. A, pp. 1–2.

8. Susan L. Crowley, "Grandparents to the Rescue," *AARP Bulletin*, vol. 34, no. 9 (October 1993), 16.

9. M. Scott Peck, *Meditations from the Road* (New York: Simon and Schuster, 1993), 21.

Chapter 2: *Children and the People Who Break Them*

1. William J. Bennett, "What to Do about the Children," *Commentary* 99, no. 3 (March 1995): 23.

2. Donna Britt, "Children's Violent Imaginings Reflect Unhealthy Society," *The* (Vancouver, Wash.) *Columbian*, 21 November 1993.

3. Ibid.

4. Ibid.

5. Karen S. Peterson, "Violent Acts Touch Many Young People," *USA Today*, 11 January 1994.

6. Brian W. Grant, *From Sin to Wholeness* (Philadelphia: Westminster Press, 1982), 10.

7. Ibid.

8. Ibid.

Chapter 4: *Parenting Pitfalls*

1. Many women I have spoken with have reported symptoms of anger, depression, and abusive behavior, which seems to coincide with hormonal changes or imbalances. For further help and information on how hormones can affect emotions see Jean Lush and Patricia H. Rushford, *The Emotional Phases of a Woman's Life* (Grand Rapids: Fleming H. Revell, 1987).

2. David Neff, "The Painless-divorce Myth," *Christianity Today* (May 12, 1989), 17.

3. Ibid.

4. *Newsweek* (December 12, 1988), 56.

5. Tom Fiche, "Preserving Chaos," *Commonweal* 122, no. 6 (March 1995): 12.

6. Janet Pais, *Suffer the Children: A Theology of Liberation by a Victim of Child Abuse* (New York: Paulist Press, 1991), 7.

7. Ibid., 10.

8. Ibid., 10, 11.

9. Andrew Vachss, "You Carry the Cure in Your Own Heart," *Parade Magazine* (August 28, 1994), 4.

Chapter 5: *The Nurturing Parent*

1. Patricia H. Rushford, "Daddy's Turn," *Christian Parenting Today* (September/October 1993), 17.

2. Adapted in part from Lloyd de Mause, ed., *The History of Childhood* (New York: Peter Bedrick Books, 1988), 6.

3. Ibid.

4. Ruth S. and C. Henry Kempe, *Child Abuse* (Cambridge, Mass.: Harvard University Press, 1978), 19–20.

5. Ibid., 20.

Chapter 6: *Do You Know How Children Grow?*

1. Gerald Corey, *Theory and Practice of Counseling and Psychotherapy*, 3rd ed. (Pacific Grove, Calif.: Brooks/Cole Publishing Company, 1977), 17.

2. Jean Illsley Clarke and Connie Dawson, *Growing Up Again* (New York: Hazelden Foundation, 1989).

3. Corey, *Theory and Practice*, 21.

4. Ibid., 18.

5. Ibid., 24.

6. Ibid., 25.

7. David Johnson and Jeff VanVonderen, *The Subtle Power of Spiritual Abuse: Recognizing and Escaping Spiritual Manipulation and False Authority within the Church* (Minneapolis: Bethany, 1991), cover copy.

8. Hannah W. Smith, *Safe within Your Love: A 40 Day Journey in the Company of Hannah W. Smith*, ed. David Hazard (Minneapolis: Bethany, 1992), 105–6.

9. William Aiken and Hugh LaFollette, eds., *Whose Child?* (Totowa, N.J.: Littlefield, Adams & Co., 1980), 41.

Chapter 7: *Reclaiming the Wonder of Childhood*

1. Vachss, "You Carry the Cure in Your Own Heart," 5.

Chapter 8: *A Place to Be*

1. Peck, *Meditations from the Road*, 20.

2. Ibid., 22.

Chapter 10: *The Difficult Child*

1. James Dobson, *The Strong-Willed Child* (Wheaton: Tyndale, 1986), 20.

2. Elizabeth DeBeasi, "The Boy inside the Whirlwind," *Christian Parenting Today* (January/February 1994), 28.

3. Paul W. Clement, "Attention Deficit Disorder," in *Baker Encyclopedia of Psychology*, ed. David G. Benner (Grand Rapids: Baker, 1985), 80–81.

4. DeBeasi, "The Boy inside the Whirlwind," 28.

5. Ibid.

6. William Kessen, "The Chinese Paradox," in Aiken and Follette, eds., *Whose Child?*, 74.

7. Ibid., 76.

8. Ibid., 78.

9. Ibid., 75–76.

10. Svea J. Gold, *When Children Invite Child Abuse* (Eugene, Ore.: Fern Ridge Press, 1986), xxii.

11. Ibid.

Chapter 11: *Plans for Parenting the Difficult Child*

1. Dobson, *The Strong-Willed Child.*

2. Bill O'Conner, "Coping with ADD," *Christian Parenting Today* (January/February, 1994), 29.

3. de Mause, ed., *The History of Childhood*, 6–7.

4. O'Conner, "Coping with ADD," 29.

Chapter 12: *Effective Discipline*

1. See Dobson, *The Strong-Willed Child*, 48.

2. Adopted from *APA Monitor* (published by the American Psychological Association) 7, no. 4 (1976).

3. With the vast changes in family structure and the increase of single-parent families, "mother" may no longer be that primary influence.

4. Gregory Bodenhamer, *Back in Control* (Englewood Cliffs, N.J.: Prentice-Hall, 1983), 11.

5. Pais, *Suffer the Children*, 130.

6. Ross Campbell, *How to Really Love Your Child* (Wheaton: Victor, 1982).

7. Adapted from Pais, *Suffer the Children*, 123–24.

8. Katherine Gordy Levine, "When Good Parents Get Angry," *Woman's Day* (September 1, 1993), 122.

9. Gary R. Collins, *Christian Counseling* (Dallas: Word, 1988), 124–25.

10. Ibid., 126.

Chapter 13: *Protecting Children from Abuse*

1. Sherryll Kerns Kraizer, *The Safe Child Book* (New York: Dell, 1985), 13–14.

2. Ibid., 16.

3. Ibid., 25–26.

4. *Crimes of the 90s*, 133.

5. Kraizer, *The Safe Child Book*, 34; *Crimes of the 90s*, 133.

6. *Crimes of the 90s*.

7. Ibid., 137.

8. Ibid., 137, 139.

9. David Foster, "Do Sex-abuse Prevention Programs Work?," *The* (Vancouver, Wash.) *Columbian*, 11 September 1994, sec. B, pp. 1, 4.

10. Ibid., B4.

11. Kraizer, *The Safe Child Book*, 45; *Crimes of the 90s*, 119.

12. *Crimes of the 90s*, 125.

13. Don Williamson, "Limiting Access to Guns Should Become a Priority," *The Oregonian*, 3 January 1994, sec. A, p. 11.

14. James Dobson, "Dr. Dobson Answers Your Questions," *Focus on the Family* (October 1993), 5.

15. Gary Gillespie, *Human Life News* (September 1994), 2.

Chapter 14: *Helping Children Help Themselves*

1. Don Oldenburg, "Adults Confronted by Memories of Abuse," *The Oregonian*, 5 July 1991.

2. Willard B. Frick, *Personality Theories: Journeys into Self* (New York and London: Teachers College Press, 1984), 15.

3. Patricia H. Rushford, *The Humpty Dumpty Syndrome: Putting Yourself Back Together Again* (Grand Rapids: Revell, 1994).

4. Lawrence Kutner, "How to Un-whine Your Child," *Parents* (May 1993), 119.

Chapter 15: *Working Together*

1. Angela Park, *Child Abuse* (New York: Glouchester Press, 1988), 19.

2. Alice Miller, *Breaking Down the Wall of Silence: The Liberating Experience of Facing Painful Truth* (New York: Dutton, 1991), 114.

3. Ibid., 116.

4. Joanne Smith and Judy Biggs, *How to Say Goodbye* (Lynnwood, Wash.: Aglow Publications, 1990), 13.

5. Jeanne M. Giovannoni and Rosina M. Becerra, *Defining Child Abuse* (New York: The Free Press, 1979), 2.

6. *What You Can Do about Child Abuse: A Guide for Mandatory Reporters* (Salem, Ore.: Children Services Division, Department of Human Resources, 1991), 14.

7. Mary Pride, *The Child Abuse Industry* (Westchester, Ill.: Crossway Books, 1986), 13. Pride cites government statistics from the American Humane Association, *Highlights of Official Child Neglect and Abuse Reporting, 1984.*

8. Pride, *The Child Abuse Industry,* 225.

9. *What You Can Do about Child Abuse,* 14.

10. Ibid., 14.

11. Ibid.

12. Eric L. Wee, *The Oregonian,* 10 May 1993, sec. C, p. 3.

13. Joyce Johnson, *What Lisa Knew: The Truth and Lies about the Steinberg Case* (New York: G. P. Putnam, 1990), 17.

14. Ibid., 303.

Chapter 16: *The Supportive Community*

1. Kathy C. Miller, *Out of Control* (Waco: Word, 1984), 18–19.

2. *Newsweek* (May 9, 1988), 74–75.

3. *Newsweek* (November 23, 1987), 70–71.

4. Nena Baker, "Don't Do as I Did," *The Oregonian,* 12 January 1994, sec. D, p. 1.

5. Bill Carey, "Strength in Family Can Ease Disputes," *The Oregonian,* 12 January 1994.

6. Johnson, *What Lisa Knew,* 16.

7. Oswald Chambers, *My Utmost for His Highest* (N.J.: Barbour and Co., 1935), 36–37.

Appendix 2: *Defining Child Abuse*

1. *What You Can Do about Child Abuse,* 57.

Appendix 3: *Guidelines for Reporting Child Abuse*

1. *What You Can Do about Child Abuse,* 9.

2. Pamela Russell and Beth Stone, *Do You Have a Secret? Adult Guide* (Minn.: CompCare Publications, 1986).

Suggested Reading List

Aiken, William, and Hugh LaFollette, eds. *Whose Child?* Totowa, N.J.: Littlefield, Adams & Co., 1980.

Anderson, Bill. *When Child Abuse Comes to Church*. Minneapolis: Bethany, 1992.

Axline, Virginia M. *Dibs in Search of Self*. New York: Ballantine, 1964. A deeply moving story of an emotionally lost child who found his way back.

———. *Play Therapy*. Rev. ed. New York: Ballantine, 1969.

Berrick, Jill Duerr, and Neil Gilbert. *With the Best of Intentions: The Child Sexual Abuse Prevention Movement*. New York: Guilford Press, 1991.

Boyd, Charles F., and David Boehi. *Different Children Different Needs: The Art of Adjustable Parenting*. Sisters, Ore.: Multnomah, 1994.

Brazo, Carol J. *No Ordinary Home: The Uncommon Art of Christ-Centered Home-Making*. Sisters, Ore.: Questar, 1995.

Campbell, Ross. *How to Really Love Your Child*. Wheaton: Victor, 1982.

———. *How to Really Love Your Teenager*. Wheaton: Victor, 1981.

Clark, Jean Illsley, and Connie Dawson. *Growing Up Again*. New York: Hazelden Foundation, 1989.

Coles, Robert. *The Spiritual Life of Children*. Boston: Houghton Mifflin, 1990.

Dobson, James. *Hide or Seek*. Rev. ed. Grand Rapids: Revell, 1979.

———. *The Strong-Willed Child*. Wheaton: Tyndale, 1986.

Endicott, Irene. *Grandparenting by Grace*. Nashville: Broadman & Holman, 1994.

———. *Grandparenting Redefined*. Lynnwood, Wash.: Aglow Publications, 1992.

Evans, Debra, ed. *Christian Parenting Answers: Before Birth to Five Years*. Colorado Springs: Christian Parenting Books, 1994. Contains works from Dr. William Sears, Dr. Grace Ketterman, V.

Gilbert Beers, Mary Manz Simon, Dr. Kay Kuzma, Patricia H. Rushford, and more.

Giesbrecht, Penny R. *Where Is God When a Child Suffers?* Hannibal: Hannibal Books, 1988.

Giovannoni, Jeanne M., and Rosina M. Becerra. *Defining Child Abuse.* New York: The Free Press, 1979.

Gold, Svea J. *When Children Invite Child Abuse.* Eugene, Ore.: Fern Ridge Press, 1986.

Grubb, W. Norton, and Marvin Lazerson. *Broken Promises: How Americans Fail Their Children.* New York: Basic Books, 1992.

Hancock, Maxine, and Karen Burton Mains. *Child Sexual Abuse: A Hope for Healing.* Wheaton: Harold Shaw, 1987.

Hunt, Gladys. *Family Secrets: What You Need to Know to Build a Strong Christian Family.* Ann Arbor, Mich.: Servant Books, 1970.

Johnson, David, and Jeff VanVonderen. *The Subtle Power of Spiritual Abuse: Recognizing and Escaping Spiritual Manipulation and False Authority within the Church.* Minneapolis: Bethany, 1992.

Kempe, Ruth S., and C. Henry. *Child Abuse.* Cambridge, Mass.: Harvard University Press, 1978.

Kraizer, Sherryll Kerns. *The Safe Child Book.* New York: Dell, 1985.

Lush, Jean, and Patricia H. Rushford. *Emotional Phases of a Woman's Life.* Grand Rapids: Revell, 1987.

de Mause, Lloyd, ed. *The History of Childhood.* New York: Peter Bedrick Books, 1988.

Miller, Alice. *Breaking Down the Wall of Silence: The Liberating Experience of Facing Painful Truth.* New York: Dutton, 1991.

Miller, Kathy C. *Out of Control.* Dallas: Word, 1984.

Pais, Janet. *Suffer the Children: A Theology of Liberation by a Victim of Child Abuse.* New York: Paulist Press, 1991.

Park, Angela. *Child Abuse.* New York: Gloucester Press, 1988.

Pride, Mary. *The Child Abuse Industry.* Wheaton: Crossway, 1986.

Rushford, Patricia H. *Have You Hugged Your Teenager Today?* Rev. ed. Grand Rapids: Revell, 1996.

———. *The Humpty Dumpty Syndrome: Putting Yourself Back Together Again.* Grand Rapids: Revell, 1994.

___. *What Kids Need Most in a Mom*. Grand Rapids: Revell, 1986.

Wallerstein, Judith, and Joan Kelley. *Surviving the Breakup*. New York: Basic Books, 1980).

Winn, Marie. *Children without Childhood: Growing Up Too Fast in a World of Sex and Drugs*. New York: Penguin, 1983.

Wright, Judy. *Kids, Chores & More: How to Get Your Kids to Help at Home*. Missoula, Mont.: Laurel 'E Press, 1994.

Wright, Norman. *Crisis Counseling*. San Bernardino, Calif.: Here's Life Publishers, 1985.

Books Parents Can Read to Children

A series of books by Doris Sanford, illustrated by Graci Evans, published by Multnomah Press, Portland, Ore.

Brian Was Adopted (1989). A boy who was adopted from Korea as an infant describes his new life in America and the love he receives from his parents.

David Has AIDS (1989). A little boy with AIDS turns to God to help him cope with the pain, fear, and loneliness that surround him.

Don't Look at Me (1986). A book about feeling different.

I Can Say No (1987). A book about drug abuse.

I Can't Talk about It (1985). At her grandmother's beach cottage, Annie reveals her father's sexual abuse of her to a dove who helps her heal and learn to trust again. Lists guidelines for adults to help sexually abused children.

I Know the World's Worst Secret (1987). A child's book about living with an alcoholic parent.

It Must Hurt a Lot (1985). A book about the death of a pet and learning and growing through the trauma.

Please Come Home (1985). A book about divorce.

A series of books by Linda Kondracki that encourages interaction of parents and children to help them understand their feelings, published by Revell, Grand Rapids.

All My Feelings Are Okay (1993).
Going Through Change Together (1996).
I Always, Always Have Choices (1992).
Let's Talk, Let's Listen Too (1993).

Other Books for Parents and Children

Dealing with Grief

Clifton, Lucille. *Everett Anderson's Goodbye.* New York: Holt, Rinehart, and Winston, 1983. Short chapters illustrate stages of grief, in this case the loss of a father.

Heegaard, Marge. *When Something Terrible Happens.* Minneapolis: Woodland Press, 1992. Deal with grief in a workbook format where the child draws and writes to identify and express his/her feelings, with help for parents.

White, E. B. *Charlotte's Web.* New York: Harper, 1952. A story of life and death, friendship and caring.

Comfort and Reassurance

Danis, Naomi. *Walk with Me.* New York: Scholastic, 1995. A toddler and a caring adult walk together in their neighborhood, experiencing sights and sounds of the outdoors. Then they return to the comfort of their house.

Joosse, Barbara M. *Mama, Do You Love Me?* San Francisco: Chronicle Books, 1991. A delightful story about a mother's unconditional love.

Kasza, Keiko. *A Mother for Choco.* New York: G. P. Putnam's Sons, 1992. Choco, a lonely bird, wishes for a mother. After meeting many animals, none of which looked like him, he finds Mrs. Bear. Even though she looks different from Choco, Mrs. Bear does all the warm comforting things that a mother would do.

McBratney, Sam. *Guess How Much I Love You.* Cambridge, Mass.: Candlewick Press, 1995. There is a deep tender bond between

Little Nutbrown Hare and Big Nutbrown Hare in this touching story that makes wonderful bedtime reading.

Payne, Lauren Murphy. *Just Because I Am: A Child's Book of Affirmation.* Minneapolis: Free Spirit Publishing, 1994.

Divorce

Brown, Larene Krasny and Marc Brown. *Dinosaurs Divorce: A Guide for Changing Families.* Boston: Atlantic Monthly Press, 1986. Reassures young children of their parents' love while it deals with the hurts and challenges of separation (ages 3–8).

Heegaard, Marge. *When Mom and Dad Separate.* Minneapolis: Woodland Press, 1991. This workbook teaches children some concepts about divorce while helping them deal with grief and focus on future good times (ages 6–11).

Krementz, Jill. *How It Feels When Parents Divorce.* New York: Alfred A. Knopf, 1992. Children from ages seven to sixteen share feelings about their parents' divorce. By listening to them, children of divorced parents learn that their own pain and anger have been experienced by others.

LeShan, Edna. *What's Going to Happen to Me?* New York: Aladdin Books, 1986. This book answers many questions that a child may have about separation and divorce (ages 8 and up).

Prokop, Michael S. *Divorce Happens to the Nicest Kids.* Warren, Ohio: Alegra House, 1986. Helps children grow in their understanding of divorce and helps them name and deal with feelings, interact with parents, and develop inner strength (ages 6–11).

Abuse and Preventative Measures

Freeman, Lory. *It's My Body.* Seattle: Parenting Press, 1982. Protective concepts are presented to young children through easily understood words and pictures. A parent's manual is available.

Freeman, Lory. *Loving Touches.* Seattle: Parenting Press, 1986. A book for all ages, but it is especially appropriate for young children as it tells through words and pictures about the need for loving touches from infancy through grandparenthood.

Hart-Rosse, Janie. *Protect Your Child from Sexual Abuse: A Parent's Guide.* Seattle: Parenting Press, 1984.

Kehoe, Patricia. *Something Happened and I'm Scared to Tell: A Book for Young Children Victims of Abuse.* Seattle: Parenting Press, 1987. Incorporates simple information, vocabulary, and emotional reassurance for even the youngest victim of sexual abuse.

Powell, E. Sandy. *Daisy.* Minneapolis: Carolrhoda Books, 1991. A sensitively written story of a nine-year-old victim of physical abuse who finds the courage to tell a trusted volunteer school tutor about her family secret.

Russell, Pamela, and Beth Stone. *Do You Have a Secret?* Minneapolis: CompCare Publications, 1986. Discusses, in simple text and illustrations, good and bad secrets, how to differentiate between them, and how not to keep bad secrets.

Library Resource Books

Books to help parents locate books on specific subjects include:

Bernstein, Joanne E. and Marsha Kabakow Rudman. *Books to Help Children Cope with Separation and Loss: An Annotated Bibliography.* New York: R. R. Bowker, 1989.

Lima, Carolyn W. *A to Zoo: Subject Access to Children's Picture Books.* 4th ed. New Providence, N.J.: R. R. Bowker, 1993.

Patricia Rushford is a speaker and an award-winning author of more than thirty books including the best-selling *What Kids Need Most in a Mom, Have You Hugged Your Teenager Today?* and *The Jennie McGrady Mystery Series.* She is also a frequent contributor to *Christian Parenting Today.* In addition she conducts writers' workshops for adults and children and is codirector of Writer's Weekend at the Beach.

Rushford is an R.N., specializing in pediatrics, and she holds a master's degree in counseling from Western Evangelical Seminary. She has two children and nine grandchildren and lives with her husband of over thirty-five years in Washington State.